NAPA VALLEY STYLE

NAPA VALLEY STYLE

Kathryn Masson

Photography by Steven Brooke

RIZZOLI
NEW YORK

Front and back cover: Italianate Farmhouse, Residence of Austin and Erika Hills (p. 118).

End papers: L'Oliveraie, Residence of Diane Morris (p. 26).

Half-title page (p. 1): Hillside vineyards at Villa Cucina above the valley.

Title page (pp. 2-3): The Beringer Winery's Rhine House, a circa 1884 neo-Gothic masterpiece, was built as the residence of Frederick Beringer.

First published in the United States of America
in 2003 by
Rizzoli International Publications, Inc.
300 Park Avenue South, New York, NY 10010
www.rizzoliusa.com

ISBN: 0-8478-2570-1
LCCN: 2003104769

Designed by Abigail Sturges

Printed and bound in the United States of America

2003 2004 2005 2006 2007 / 10 9 8 7 6 5 4 3 2 1

To Carter Lowrie and Bill Ryan;
to my husband David Pashley;
and

to Robert and Margrit Mondavi.

CONTENTS

Preceding pages: Sutter Home Winery's circa 1884 Victorian house serves as guest headquarters for the Trinchero family-owned enterprise.

Right: The Niebaum-Coppola Estate Winery, designed in 1884 by William Mooser, has undergone a complete restoration by current owners Eleanor and Francis Ford Coppola.

The Napa Valley, just an hour north of San Francisco, is a world-famous destination for wine lovers, gourmands, and vacationers. Eclectic architecture within its vineyards offers a visual history of the valley's development and conveys the spirit and soul of its creators. The Napa Valley is a perfect place to grow grapes, and, over a relatively short period of time, pioneers, artists, and entrepreneurs have helped to create an American culture that values fine wine. This success has brought wealth to the valley and a mystique that it epitomizes "the good life." By melding Old World traditions with modern sensibilities, those who live here have enriched the natural landscape with homes that celebrate a vision for that "good life," full of energy and affirmation. This book presents the spirit and beauty of a select group of these residences.

EARLY HISTORY

Among the many valleys of the northern Coast Range of California, the Napa Valley has unique natural features. Drained by the Napa River, the valley is at a low elevation, terminating at sea level at San Pablo Bay. Its low elevation and relatively low latitude reduce the frequency of frosts, while its breadth and gentle southward slope have resulted in deposits of deep, rich alluvial soils. The word "Napa" refers to a type of village in the languages of the Wappo and Patwin (or Southern Wintu) nations, the last Native Americans to live in the valley before the arrival of Europeans.

These people, who left no architectural monuments, virtually succumbed to oppressive treatment and smallpox by the 1860s.

European settlement began after the Napa Valley was used to graze cattle for Solana de San Francisco (est. 1823). The northernmost of the California missions, it was located to the west in what was to become the town of Sonoma. George C. Yount was the first Anglo to receive a land grant in the Napa Valley, 12,000 acres awarded in 1836 as payment for carpentry work at the mission in Sonoma. His Rancho Caymus encompassed what is now Yountville, Oakville, and Rutherford. He raised livestock and crops, including the valley's first grapes from which he produced the first Napa Valley wine. Yount also constructed Napa's first wooden house, a Kentucky blockhouse, eighteen feet square and two stories high. Edward T. Bale secured the 17,000-acre land grant to the north, which extended from what is now Rutherford through St. Helena to Calistoga. Both Yount and Bale built sawmills and gristmills and provided shelter and sustenance for traveling mountain men and new settlers. Their crude log cabins were later replaced by more substantial residences constructed of milled lumber from surrounding redwood and oak groves. In subsequent years, the community of Napa City grew up at a tidal ford in the Napa River a few miles north of San Pablo Bay. By 1848, the Napa Valley was home to about thirty families.

The Culinary Institute of America at Greystone was originally the W. B. Bourn Wine Cellar, c. 1889.

THE GOLD RUSH
TO THE TURN OF THE CENTURY

California's history changed dramatically in 1848 when the land was wrested from Mexico by the United States and gold was discovered in the western foothills of the Sierra Nevada. An influx of fortune-seeking adventurers expanded the City of Napa instantaneously, filling the town with miners who over-wintered in its mild climate in makeshift canvas and redwood houses or wood-frame hotels and patronized the many bars and brothels. The growing city's community and commercial buildings were constructed of redwood and oak, supplemented occasionally with brick or stone, in a simple rural style typical of Western towns of the era.

After the Gold Rush, European settlers began the first serious commercial wine production in the Napa Valley. Buena Vista Winery, founded by Hungarian Agoston Haraszthy in 1857 in the neighboring Sonoma Valley, was the first winery in Northern California. Haraszthy sold some vineyard property in Sonoma to Charles Krug, a young German with whom he had been sharing his knowledge of viticulture. When Krug married the daughter of Edward Bale in 1860, he received more than three hundred acres on which he planted vineyards and built Napa's first commercial winery, an impressive three story cellar of wood and stone. Thereafter,

wineries proliferated in the valley, and the jubilant way of life of early European vintners set an Old World cultural tone. Many buildings of local limestone and a pale volcanic rock survive today, a tribute to fine craftsmanship and Old World design.

A majority of the domestic architecture at the time was simply constructed in a typically Western, clapboard "ranch" style with Victorian detailing. Over the next two decades, however, increasingly affluent Napa Valley residents began to commission European-trained architects to design more ornate Victorian buildings that reflected their wealth and social standing and emulated the fashionable styles of San Francisco. Two late-nineteenth-century commercial stone buildings notable for their Romanesque features remain. One of them, the former Inglenook Winery, is a majestic chateau designed for sea captain Gustave Niebaum in the early 1880s by Swiss architect William Mooser. Meticulously restored by the current owners, Eleanor and Francis Ford Coppola, it is now the Niebaum-Coppola Estate Winery. The other was originally the W.B. Bourn Wine Cellar, now the Culinary Institute of America. Designed in 1889 by George W. Percy and F. F. Hamilton, architects who were originally from Maine, it is considered one of the finest Romanesque-style buildings in the West. Residential architecture of the period also bore a strong European influence, best seen in the Rhine

House, the mansion of Frederick Beringer, which was designed by architect Albert Schroepfer in 1884 as a re-creation of the Beringer family seat in Mainz.

The wine industry ebbed and flowed during the last three decades of the nineteenth century. Booms led to over expansion and failure, and periodic phylloxera epidemics attacked the vines. By the turn of the century, many grape growers had abandoned their wineries, turning to walnut and prune production. At the same time, however, publication of books, scientific studies, and how-to manuals bolstered America's confidence in the largely misunderstood wine culture.

The industry rebounded after 1900 with introduction of the phylloxera-resistant Rupestris St. George rootstock. California vintners improved their wine to compete with European products, and their wines gained credibility both in restaurants and at international exhibitions. Writers sought to enlighten the public about the relationship between wine and food, promoting wine as the temperance beverage that encouraged moderation. The wine industry in the Napa Valley was on the mend. In the meantime, however, alchohol abuse had aroused a righteous Protestant nation, culminating in passage of the Volstead Act in 1919, which outlawed alcoholic beverages in America.

PROHIBITION

Prohibition brought shock and dismay to the Napa Valley. Wineries disposed of their inventory and were shut by federal agents. Some growers converted to production of cider or grape juice, or planted cotton, rice, or fruit and nut trees. Beringer Vineyards stayed solvent by dehydrating grapes into raisins, packing them into bricks, and selling them with instructions for reconstitution into wine. Greystone and Beaulieu made sacramental wine for the Catholic Church. Many small wineries remained in business undetected, filling the empty jugs of weekend partiers from San Francisco. Most wineries with mortgages failed, and their vines grew wild or died. By 1928, beer and hard liquor had become the alcoholic beverages of choice. In the frenzied pace of modernism, American society had left the slow delights of wine behind. The Napa Valley lost its raison d'être and the wine industry had reached rock bottom. For decades, even after repeal in 1933, there were more than a hundred abandoned nineteenth-century stone wineries and thousands of fallow acres in the Napa Valley.

RESURGENCE

In the early 1930s, orchards of plums, cherries, apricots, pears, peaches, apples, walnuts, figs, and olives dominated the Napa Valley. The population grew slowly in the relaxed, rural California setting. But the wine industry was reviving as the valley's reputation for consistently good wine grew.

Beaulieu, Inglenook, Beringer, and others took medals at fairs and exhibitions. By 1937 forty wineries had twenty thousand acres planted to vines.

Ambitious winegrowers such as Louis M. Martini, who had built his winery in 1934, were eager to achieve premier status for Napa Valley's wines. In the late 1930s two men helped usher in the modern era of wine making: the now legendary Russian André Tchelistcheff, winemaker for Georges de Latour at Beaulieu, and John Daniels, grand-nephew of Gustave Niebaum, who became marketing and sales director of Inglenook. These men upgraded California wines with innovation, expertise, and experimentation. A dearth of European products during World War II brought brand-name Napa Valley wines before the public eye. Shortly after the war, the Napa Valley Vintners Association was formed to upgrade and promote the valley's wine. Wineries such as Krug, Beringer, Louis M. Martini, and Christian Brothers began to make premium wines that competed with the finest European products and gained a larger share of the American market. But the fickle nature of American tastes continued to torment the winegrowers of the Napa Valley. It was Ernest and Julio Gallo, a wine company from the Central Valley, that kept these wineries afloat during most of the 1950s and 1960s. Gallo bought sixty to seventy-five percent of all of the wine made in Napa, Sonoma, and

Mendicino counties and resold it in wider circles than the smaller wineries' limited distribution channels could reach.

American interest in wine grew during the 1960s along with the popularity of gourmet food. An increasingly affluent public was ready for "the good life," of which wine was an integral part. Among the vintners who most passionately believed in the promotion of Napa Valley's wines were Louis P. Martini, André Tchelistcheff, Robert and Peter Mondavi (who, together, had owned and run Krug since 1947), Leland Stewart, the Jack Taylors, and Legh Knowles of Beaulieu. Robert Mondavi left Krug in 1966 to start his own enterprise. Committed to this promotion, he held conferences, special events, and lectures across America and Europe, speaking about the close relationship of food and wine and inspiring the public to live differently, better, more completely. These activities earned him the friendly title "Baron

of the Valley." Special charity events such as the Annual Wine Auction, started by Robert Mondavi with his wife Margrit in 1981, promoted tourism. Wine tasting bars were opened in wineries, facilities were enlarged to hold cultural events such as music concerts and art exhibitions, and new wineries were built with architecture that caught the traveler's eye.

During an incredible boom in the 1970s, twenty-four thousand acres were planted to vines. In 1976, a blind tasting in Paris put the Napa Valley permanently on the map. Gold medals were won by winemakers Mike Grgich (now of Grgich Hills Winery) for his Chateau Montelena Chardonnay and Warren Winiarski for his Cabernet Sauvignon from Stag's Leap Wine Cellars. There was no turning back. The wealthy and adventurous from all parts of the world invested in vineyards and new wineries and changed the profile of the modern vintner.

The Chateau Montelena Winery's design was based on the great chateaux of the Bordeaux region in France.

The Napa Opera House, c. 1879, located in downtown Napa, is a Napa County Landmark. It serves as a center for performing arts and special events.

The boom continued into the 1980s and 1990s. Appellations were designated and micro-climates and soil types became intensely relevant. Napa Valley became world renowned, attracting overwhelming numbers of visitors and new residents, which in turn spurred the opening of a multitude of fine restaurants and up-scale resorts, spas, and bed and breakfasts. The impact of this rapid growth prompted the formation of grass roots organizations that became the valley's conscience. The Napa County Landmarks and the Napa County Historical Society were formed to promote the preservation of the area's architectural heritage while the Napa Valley Foundation seeks to maintain the agricultural and small-town character of the county. In 1982, the Board of Supervisors developed a long-range plan for preserving open space, limiting residential development, and reducing hillside erosion.

TODAY

Napa Valley residents now strive to maintain the valley's special relaxed charm and country ambiance amidst over 250 wineries and more than 2 million visitors a year. The valley's principal settlements are the City of Napa and three smaller towns to the north, Yountville, St. Helena, and Calistoga, each a vital part of the valley's history and each maintaining a distinct character.

The City of Napa is now an urban center that retains the aura of a small country town, due largely to its charming Victorian architecture. Important restored commercial buildings in the historic district and more than three hundred Victorian houses represent a full spectrum of styles. Restoration of important historic landmark structures continues to enhance the architectural allure of Napa. The Napa Opera

Above: The four-star Napa River Inn is the centerpiece of the restored Hatt Building, c. 1884, at the Historic Napa Mill. The complex has restaurants, a European bakery, a gourmet market, and a Greenhaus Spa.

Left: Guestrooms at the Napa River Inn are plush and elegant. The Inn was given the President's Award for Excellence by the California Preservation Foundation in 2003. Photo by Dennis Anderson.

House, c. 1879, and the Hatt Building, c. 1884, at the Napa Mill, are central to the city's transformation and its promotion of culture and the arts. The nineteenth-century mill complex has been fully restored and adapted for use as the intimate Napa River Inn and its marketplace.

Exciting contemporary projects that have contributed to the downtown renaissance include the Oxbow School, designed by Stanley Saitowitz. Perhaps the most ambitious and significant project is COPIA: The American Center for Wine, Food, & the Arts designed by the Polshek Partnership. Robert Mondavi conceived and supported this museum and cultural center, which presents a fascinating array of programs and exhibits integrating the arts with food and wine. The ambitious twenty-year Napa River Flood Protection Project, begun in 1998, and the Napa

The elegant Victorian town of St. Helena in the middle of the Napa Valley maintains its bygone-era charm, though filled with fine restaurants and stylish boutiques.

Urban Waterfront Restoration Plan, will ensure downtown Napa's on-going revival.

Original settler George Yount was renowned for goodwill and hospitality, and Yountville must have absorbed much of his élan and generosity. Today, the charming hamlet boasts the largest number of restaurants per capita in the United States, many renowned in gourmet circles. The former Gottlieb Groezinger Winery complex, which dominates the center of town, now houses such restaurants as the casual California-style Pacific Blues Café. This mid-valley cross-roads, once a haven for bootleggers, remains surprisingly quaint and quiet.

Farther up the valley, St. Helena arose because of natural hot springs and a salubrious climate. The White Sulphur Springs resort, a hotel and restaurant built in 1852, led to a building boom in the small township of Hot Springs. Later renamed St. Helena, the town became a luxurious seasonal retreat for San Francisco's elite. Many well-preserved, late-nineteenth-century buildings maintain the town's prosperous Victorian flavor.

Still farther north, Calistoga also developed around natural hot springs. Sam Brannan, San Francisco's first newspaper publisher, a wealthy, energetic entrepreneur, and an often unscrupulous opportunist, saw this former Wappo health retreat as his ticket to millionaire status. Brannan

Right: Calistoga reflects the typical architecture of a small Western town.

Below: Cakebread Cellars in Rutherford was established in 1973. The winery was originally designed by William Turnbull, with later additions by Don Brandenburger.

dreamed of creating a great resort spa, a Saratoga of California. An inebriated malapropism turned the name into Calistoga. By the time the resort opened in 1862, Brannan had spent his fortune on twenty-five ornate Victorian cottages, a gigantic reservoir, a racetrack and stables, and other amenities of a world-class spa. Success was fleeting, and, by 1873, Brannan was bankrupt. Shortly thereafter, most of the town was divided up and sold as individual parcels. Fires in 1901 and 1907 caused much destruction, but the town was rebuilt by a conscientious community. Calistoga thrives today, its architecture representing a typical, charming early twentieth-century Western town.

Right: Opus One was designed by Paul Johnson. The winery was begun as a joint venture between Robert Mondavi and the late Baron Philippe de Rothchild of France.

Below: Clos Pegase Winery is the award-winning design of architect Michael Graves.

Visitors to the Napa Valley come for the fine food and wine, the serenity, and the evocative landscape and architecture forever intertwined with the valley's history. Some distinctive Victorian winery buildings, such as Beringer and Sutter Home, capture the essence of an era. Sharing the spotlight are modern works such as Cakebread Cellars by William Turnbull, and contemporary buildings such as Clos Pegase by Michael Graves, Opus One by Paul Johnson, and Dominus by the Swiss architects Jacques Herzog and Pierre de Meuron. These additions to the valley's built environment have become important milestones in its development, representing the diversity, individuality, and good taste of its vintners, the keepers of the valley.

The history, creativity, and personal styles

of the wineries are also evident in the
variety and eclecticism of the valley's
residential architecture. The following essays
and photographs show the tremendous
exuberance and immense diversity in how
people live and thrive here. The architecture and gardens are as individual as
their owners, and all convey, in their own
way, the joy and blessedness each resident
feels in calling the Napa Valley home.

Preceding pages: A pergola filters light onto the spacious outdoor dining area that easily seats thirty guests at L'Oliveraie. Original stone walls of the former winery building add character to the spectacular setting.

Right: Expertise in eighteenth-century French architecture is evident in architect Andrew Skurman's design for the estate's carriage house. Skurman, an authority on neo-classical architecture, has perfectly integrated the new structure with the existing estate buildings.

A visit to L'Oliveraie immediately conjures up a single word: Perfection. Others follow: serenity, harmony, loveliness, and grace. These qualities are palpable throughout the eleven-acre estate in Rutherford, which was developed as a winery in the 1880s. Today, the main house, originally the stone winery, is a contemporary interpretation of a French manor house, surrounded by formal gardens, olive groves, and seven acres of vineyards.

This abundant beauty is the result of Diane Morris's careful orchestration of myriad artful and well-planned details. Secrets to her success include a clear vision, an impeccable eye, and a talented team of gardeners, designers, and an overseer who share her refined sensibilities and passion for the property.

In 1987 architects Porter & Steinwidel began to transform the historic but decaying winery into a residence. Stone walls were preserved both as structural elements and as integral features of the interior design. Subsequently, guest cottages and a carriage house were added, designed in an architectural vocabulary that complements the main house. The carriage house, designed by San Francisco architect Andrew Skurman, is the first significant architectural element visible through the vineyard. Skurman, an authority on neoclassical design, skillfully incorporated

Above: The southernmost portion of the backyard is a symphony in shades of green—a brilliant lawn edged with a series of boxwood spheres borders a vast vineyard at the base of the Mayacamas Mountains.

Right: At the entrance to L'Oliveraie, the muted tones of Provence lavender, aged olive trees, and stone walls complement bolder landscape elements such as finely shaped boxwood, the crisp white petals of seasonally changed flora, and an espalier of Magnolia with rich green leaves.

Right: The potager provides fresh vegetables and fruit year round. Its design recalls gardens of the French countryside in the eighteenth century.

Below: An antique French fountain serves as the focal point for an exquisite smaller garden with parterres of trimmed boxwood.

an extant water tower into the new building, a design that sets the tone for the estate beyond. "The new carriage house recalls the historic manor language," he explains. "True to its historical precedent, the building is modest yet elegant and carefully detailed, integrating well with the French character of the property."

The impressive gardens of L'Oliveraie, laid out by landscape architect Walter Guthrie, reflect the formal, axial designs of the great eighteenth-century French country gardens. Claudia Schmidt, a garden designer based in the Napa Valley, chose the plantings and continues to advise on seasonal changes. Overseer John Hallman maintains the estate with meticulous attention to detail. For example, to espalier Fuji apple trees against a fence, he made ties from pale gray leather to blend with the green-gray wood. When asked why he went to such trouble, he

Below: The entrance hall contains a display of eighteenth-century French Pont aux Choux faience above a sixteenth-century Louis XIII sofa covered in embroidered linen, with "os de mouton" legs.

Right: In the living room, arrangements of eighteenth-century French farm tools complement the rustic stone walls, while refined features include the fireside coffee table, an eighteenth-century French steel tray with pierced gallery on a custom base, a sofa table of bronze and granite from the Paris studio of Philippe Anthonioz, a rare nineteenth-century Anglo-Indian tea caddy of horn and ivory, and a Han jar converted into a lamp with pewter-leafed mounts and trim.

replied with a huge smile, "We all have fun here, from the owner on down."

The peaceful exterior palette of greens, grays, lavenders, and white has been brought inside the house by interior designer C. Terrence Schell, who is based in San Francisco. Schell's goal of allowing the architecture to speak is achieved by emphasizing the original stone walls and selecting authentic elements—furniture, decorative objects, and custom pieces—that are either eighteenth-century French or compatible in design. His deep knowledge and understanding of the period and his philosophy that "aesthetics are the easiest way to nurture" have created a comfortable, elegant setting that delights all of the senses as well as the spirit.

Residence of Diane Morris
Circa 1880 Winery
1987 Main residence; Porter & Steinwidel, Architects
1999 Carriage House; Andrew Skurman, Architect

YORK-ALEXANDER HOUSE

Preceding pages: The south façade of the original portion of the historic York Alexander House contains a charming sun porch enclosed at a later date with evocative fenestration.

Right: The main entrance of the house boasts Victorian Italianate design details such as heavy wooden corbels and stone piers and engaged pilasters.

Following pages: The residence is graced with a park-like setting that includes an expansive lawn and many grand trees from the late nineteenth century.

The historic York-Alexander house, as it is called in official documents of the State of California, is a direct link with the Napa Valley's earliest settlers. As one of very few stone residences dating from the building boom of the 1870s, it is also one of the most significant structures in the valley. Its distinctive Italianate style, with a characteristic deep, overhanging roof supported by scrolled corbels, as well as the unusual carved stonework at the entry and on the arched window and door surrounds, make the York-Alexander house one of Napa Valley's most splendid Victorian homes.

Eli McLean York built the house and a stone winery (see p. 44), known as the York Winery or York Cellars, about 1877 on a ten-acre lot in St. Helena. Eli and his brother Andrew arrived in California after "working their way across the American plains driving seven hundred head of cattle and fifty head of mules and horses," according to the 1902 publication *Historical and Biographical Record* and research by John York, a current St. Helena resident. Both brothers started wineries, Eli in St. Helena, and Andrew in San Luis Obispo. Silas York, Eli's son, inherited the St. Helena property. It subsequently passed to his sister's heirs, the C.L. Alexander family, who lived there until the early 1900s. Records show that the estate remained intact until 1957 when the land was divided into two five-acre parcels, each with a stone structure.

The York-Alexander house has been enlarged, most significantly by a substantial east wing, but it is still full of the grace and charm of the nineteenth century. Indigenous materials such as fieldstone and wood have been used to complement the original structure. A guest house and tennis court were added in the 1990s.

John Berggruen, owner of John Berggruen Gallery in San Francisco, and his wife, Gretchen, escape to this country house as often as they can. Well-chosen pieces of contemporary art—masks, paintings, sculpture—add color and movement to the simple forms and mellow tones of the interior. This eclectic collection is successfully juxtaposed with traditional and antique furniture. The living and dining rooms retain handsome, original details, and the views over the park-like setting evoke the nineteenth century. The house has evolved through time with its various owners, including the Berggruens, yet the integrity of the historic building is intact, preserving an important part of the heritage of the Napa Valley.

Residence of John and Gretchen Berggruen
Stone Italianate Residence, c. 1877

Above: A corner of the living room reveals the interior's clean lines and smooth surfaces that complement the Berggruens' collection of contemporary art.

Right: A large farm table fills the dining room's sunlit space.

E. YORK WINE CELLAR

Below: A contemporary addition in cement and steel houses a sitting room and office.

Right: The living room integrates diverse art such as "Red Shoes," a figural sculpture by David Hostetler, three early-twentieth-century Chinese-red chests, and a 1981 painting by Christopher Brown.

Marion Greene has owned the former E. York Wine Cellar for nearly thirty years. Located north of St. Helena, the winery building and an Italianate stone house (see p. 36) were built in 1877 by Eli McLean York, who had come to California from the Midwest. Today both structures, each on half of the original ten-acre lot, are used as residences, still surrounded by open countryside.

The San Francisco firm of Kuth/Ranieri Architects converted the hip-roofed stone warehouse structure into an expansive home and office complex. On the upper level are the private quarters while the ground floor contains offices, a large conference area, and gallery space. At the southwest corner, the architects added a contemporary concrete tower that houses a sitting room on the residential level and an office below. This contemporary architectural form and a geometrically patterned, curved steel balcony above the entrance are juxtaposed with the style and materials of the historic building to create a provocative tension between old and new.

On the interior, a series of interventions have had a comparable effect. The original small windows in the thick stone walls admit only minimal light, but an ingenious solution has now opened the rooms to substantial sunlight. A continuous band of skylights inserted below the base of the overhanging roofline creates a clerestory

A John Dickinson dining room table creates a smooth transition into the kitchen where contemporary chrome and steel appliances juxtapose dramatically with the indigenous stone walls of the original warehouse.

at the top of the interior stone walls. More light is added with a reflective all-white ceiling. Throughout the space, huge, new smooth-finished structural beams intersect with rustic wooden beams of the original structure. Bleached wood floors with a high gloss finish abut the rough stone walls. These new elements create an exciting visual impact that plays the modern against the historic and provides the perfect setting for the owner's art collection. The open plan based on adjacencies rather than partitions allows freedom of movement and flexible space for the display of colorful contemporary paintings, wall hangings, and sculpture as well as carved and painted antique pieces. The collection ranges from works by San Francisco artist Armando Rascon and New York painter Nancy Spero to unusual tin finials from a late-nineteenth-century barn and a sixteenth-century Spanish polychromed-wood figure.

The building's historic character is so strong that modern architectural interventions have only corrected flaws that had kept the structure from being livable. The original stone structure remains an important reminder of the early history of the Napa Valley, and its maintenance and preservation are more essential to the built landscape of the valley each year.

Residence of Marion Greene
Stone Winery, c. 1877

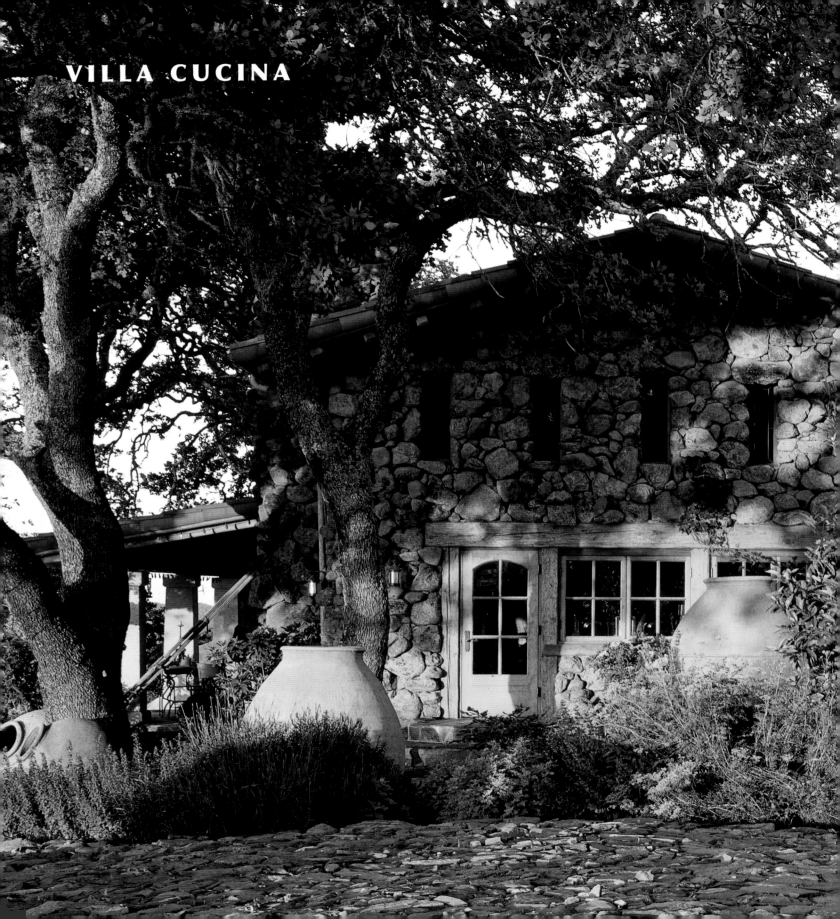

VILLA CUCINA

Preceding pages: Heavy boulders and timber salvaged from the vineyard sites give the monumental Villa Cucina its Old World charm.

Right: The primo relaxation spot in the backyard affords a vista of Lake Hennessey and the Napa Valley.

A rare and powerful quixotic spirit drives food and wine connoisseur Pat Kuleto, who masterminds an astounding array of commercial and artistically creative endeavors in San Francisco and at his home, Villa Cucina, in the eastern hills near Rutherford overlooking Lake Hennessey and the Napa Valley. Renowned as the creator of some of the Bay area's most dramatic and fabulous restaurants, Kuleto has garnered multiple awards for their design as well as their food and wine. His latest enterprise, however, focuses on his long-standing love of making fine wine. To this end, he has recently added a winery to his hilltop property, built near the rustic country villa in a complementary style with similar materials.

The architecture of this compound, conceived by Kuleto, has a monumental Old World character. Massive buildings, constructed of indigenous stone and timber salvaged from the site as the vineyards were planted, are bold interpretations of a grand lodge and wine cellar with a conscious blending of allusions to Mediterranean and early California precedents. A spectacular presence amid lush flower and vegetable gardens, the villa also conveys the basic comforts of early California craftsman-style cottages in its form, massing, and use of natural materials. Walls of boulders that have been mounded and piled to support low-slung roofs of hand-adzed logs have a pleasing earthiness and stability.

Inside the home that Kuleto shares with his
son, Daniel, is a multi-level space that
includes family quarters, guestrooms, and
offices, all accessed by winding staircases or
turns from short hallways. The great room
that dominates the main floor is perfect for
entertaining. There are multiple dining and
conversation areas, including a huge stone
hearth surrounded by deep sofas. An extra
long galley-style kitchen features various
ovens and a thick wooden counter used for
preparation and serving. Low lighting sheds
a warm glow on natural textures and a
maze of colorful furnishings and decorative
accents. A glazed tile mosaic, hand-woven
rugs from Morocco patterned with natural
dyes, worn leather chairs draped with
exotic textiles, and chunky, carved wood
tables and chairs fill the space. Custom-
designed hand-blown glass lamps punctuate
the scene with small but powerful touches
of deep cobalt blue.

At Villa Cucina, an abundance of what
makes entertaining great is produced on
the property. A hillside of cutting gardens
provides fresh flowers daily, hedges of caper
berries are plucked to garnish appetizer
trays, and a large vegetable garden produces
healthy stock to accompany entrees
expertly prepared and paired, of course,
with the right Kuleto Estate Family
Vineyards vintage. By the pool and tucked
in the gardens are seating areas where
guests may enjoy the vistas of the
vineyards, rugged mountain terrain, and

the valley and lake below. These eight hundred acres in California's pristine foothills, one hundred or more of them planted with selections of grape varietals, is now as imposing a ranch as any carved out by the first fearless pioneers.

Residence of Pat Kuleto, 1995
Dave Berman, Architect
Pat Kuleto, Architectural Designer

Hand-hewn beams and a plethora of copper, iron, and well-patinaed wood, including a ten-foot antique European chopping block, give this state-of-the-art kitchen its glorious atmosphere.

Following pages: The view of Lake Hennessey from Villa Cucina.

Pages 60–61: Kuleto prefers the taste of grapes stressed from growth on the steep rocky hillsides.

THE LANGTRY HOUSE

Preceding pages: The Lillie Langtry ranch house, c. 1880, is now part of Guenoc and Langtry Estate Vineyards and Winery, owned by the Magoon family.

Below: A copy of one of the portraits of Lillie Langtry hangs over a piano that she reportedly once owned.

Right: A scene from the porch of the farmhouse notes portions of the vast landholdings of Guenoc Winery that are partially planted to vineyards.

Who would not have the same reaction as the legendary beauty Lillie Langtry at first sight of this simple Victorian ranch house set in the vast, pristine Guenoc Valley? Her words, telegraphed to the attorney who had acquired the property for her, convey an awe that is still felt today: "Am delighted. Words don't express my complete satisfaction. Join me in Paradise."

When Lillie Langtry came to San Francisco in 1884 on her first tour of America, she fell in love with the West. At 31, Langtry was already an international celebrity, both as a performer and as a sophisticated woman of the world. California offered an allure and opportunities that her native England lacked. Originally she planned to live at least six months out of every year on her 4,200-acre farm, managing vineyards and partnering with Freddie Gebhard, a wealthy "American friend." His Guenoc Stock Farm, a Thoroughbred breeding operation, and her ranch and wine business, Langtry Farms, were quickly recognized for outstanding products.

By the early 1900s, the Guenoc Valley was known for fine wines. In collaboration with a winemaker from Bordeaux, Langtry achieved her goal of producing the finest claret in America. Labels on the bottles featured her likeness, based on her portrait by the British artist George Frederick Watts. Even after she and Gebhard were no longer a team, Langtry—now an absentee owner, who was regularly away travelling—continued to manage and expand her estate working with a ranch manager and adding gardens and several smaller out buildings. Her successful vineyards supported six winery buildings, whose foundations still exist. She owned the property for eighteen years, only selling it in 1906 because of tight finances.

The land today, now reincorporated into the 21,000-acre Mexican land grant property of 1845, is owned by the Magoon family. These preservation and conservation minded individuals are deeply respectful of the heritage of which they have become stewards. Beginning in the early 1960s when they acquired the land, the Magoons carefully researched the historic property and restored the modest farmhouse to its late-nineteenth-century ambiance.

The Magoons have revived Langtry's winery operation after more than half a century of dormancy. As the owners of Guenoc and Langtry Estate Vineyards and Winery, the Magoons consistently produce award-winning vintages. The house and its idyllic setting bordering the northernmost edge of Napa County remains one of the most beautiful sites in America. With its rugged hills and ridges and its lush valley floor planted to

vines, its resources are developed in the most benign way, leaving its rural character untouched. Thanks to environmentalist, farmer, and winegrower Orville Magoon, this serene landscape is preserved for generations to come.

Tours by appointment.

Magoon Family Residence, c. 1880
Victorian Ranch House

From the Guenoc Winery a pastoral view includes vineyards and the historic Langtry House in the distance.

SPOTTSWOODE

The focal point of the historic Spottswoode estate is one of the most charming Victorian farmhouses built in the Napa Valley. The two-story, clapboard house, completed in 1885, is set on forty acres of vineyards against the low-lying backdrop of the Mayacamas Mountains. Immediately adjacent are six acres of original landscaping with slender palm trees, two-hundred-year-old native oaks, and a profusion of flowering vines and shrubs. Today the property is owned and operated by Mary Novak, who also owns and operates Spottswoode Winery.

Originally called Esmeralda, the house was built as a summer retreat by George Schonewald, a St. Helena resident who was the first general manager of the sumptuous Hotel Del Monte in Monterey. In designing his house, Schonewald drew on architectural elements of the Del Monte, particularly in the details of the raised porch, which incorporates identical circular ornament. Known in its heyday as "the most elegant seaside resort in the world," the Hotel Del Monte was built by the owners of the Southern Pacific Railroad to promote travel to the West. It was located on holdings of more 20,000 acres that include today's Pebble Beach and portions of the Carmel Valley. Among the unusual amenities were the 17-Mile Drive created to take guests through the scenic hillside forest to the Carmel mission, a luxurious grand bathhouse, and a mile-long racetrack with grandstand.

Left: Touches of Victorian elegance are found throughout the nineteenth-century farmhouse.

Right: Magnificent stained glass windows in the double front doors imbue the entrance with charm.

In the Napa Valley, Schonewald established a vineyard and became a real estate investor. Following his tenure at the Del Monte, he continued his career in hotel management at the Palace in San Francisco and the Coronado in San Diego. When he moved away in 1906, he sold his Napa Valley holdings, including Esmeralda. Subsequent owners, Mr. and Mrs. Albert Spotts, renamed the property Spottswoode in 1910.

Mary Novak and her late husband, Jack, bought the property in 1972, intending to become viticulturists and vintners. The Novaks undertook the painstaking work of replanting the vineyards and restored the farmhouse. Aware of its historical significance, they captured the attic space for bedrooms without changing the exterior configuration. In 1982 Spottswoode Winery produced its first vintage.

These early efforts have come to fruition in the vineyards and at home, for which Mary Novak feels extremely fortunate. The five Novak children who grew up in the farmhouse return frequently with their own children to enjoy the welcoming atmosphere, and three daughters are involved in the Spottswoode Winery, ensuring its future as a successful family business.

Residence of Mary Novak, c. 1885
Victorian Farmhouse

ARAUJO ESTATE HOUSE

As proprietors of Araujo Estate Wines and the renowned Eisele Vineyard, Bart and Daphne Araujo have deep roots in the most basic element of land. Bart, whose family includes generations of ranchers from Northern California, longed to return to its rural environment. Daphne, an Army officer's daughter who spent her earliest years in the beautiful countryside of Virginia and Pennsylvania, had become a landscape architect. In 1990 the couple left careers in Southern California and moved to the Napa Valley, where they bought a 160-acre Calistoga estate. Undaunted by the long-term commitment that wine growers make to the land (a minimum of seven years from planting to produce a wine), the Araujos proceeded to replant the vineyard, reestablish the olive grove, and renovate the estate buildings.

An extant barn, built about 1860, provided the contextual direction for the overall project. The scope included use of a portion of the barn for new offices, renovation of the clapboard guesthouses, design of a new redwood winery and cellar complex, and the construction of a new two-story house on the footprint of the original residence.

Ned Forrest of Forrest Architects in Sonoma designed the house, working closely with Daphne Araujo to incorporate a sense of southern graciousness in its proportions and detailing. The two-story form, a sweeping front porch, and wood siding with shuttered windows, respect the rural history of the Napa Valley and, to Araujo's trained eye, "fit comfortably and appropriately into its context." Pecan wood floors of a medium tone and wide cream-colored crown moldings complement the traditional furnishings, soft palette of fabrics, and fine collection of nineteenth-century California landscape paintings. A band of windows and French doors opening to the south fill the rooms with a calming, mild light. Adjacent to the house is an exquisite parterre herb garden.

Equal attention was paid to the other gardens and the forty-acre vineyard, which are farmed organically and bio-dynamically.

Below: The fine woodwork and detailing of the living room establish a fairly stylized and formal interior.

Bottom : The dining room is appointed with fine Dresden China. When larger facilities are needed, the winery-cave is opened and guests are seated among the oak wine barrels.

Right: The serene library affords views of the surrounding hills, specialty gardens, and olive groves.

The landscape includes a large vegetable garden, a backyard hillside planted with native species, herbs, and flowers, and two hundred producing olive trees. Regarding the organically farmed vineyard, Daphne notes, "If your perspective is long range, it is a more thoughtful and responsible way to garden."

There is no harshness or sharp corner in the Araujo establishment. Its perfection, like their internationally acclaimed wines, is attributable to a belief in the land and pleasure in the livelihood it provides. "Farmers learn humility from the land. We have to accept that we're not in control and that there's a new and wonderful environment that is bigger than we are. We also learn patience because we're in a long term situation," Daphne explains. "But it's extremely satisfying to know that you are giving others pleasure and to be a part of such a stimulating international community." The Araujos have made a substantial contribution to the tradition of the Napa Valley, not only producing a world-class wine in an ecologically sensitive manner, but also restoring a beautiful California homestead worthy of its idyllic setting.

Residence of Bart and Daphne Araujo, 1999
Ned Forrest, Architect

TYCHSON HILL

Preceding pages: Tychson Hill, with its nineteenth-century ambiance, was designed as a rural farmhouse.

Right: The landscape plan is perfectly attuned to the historic vision for the property.

Ann Colgin and her husband Joe Wender are visionaries with historical perspective. Colgin, an antiquarian and art expert who has worked at both Christie's and Sotheby's, bought the nineteenth-century house and adjacent vineyards of Josephine Tychson, the first woman winemaker in California. A savvy business woman and vintner whose fine wines have won accolades throughout the industry since 1992, Colgin has restored the original vineyards and is building a state-of-the-art winery on the property. Wender, an advisory director at Goldman Sachs in Los Angeles, has contributed his expertise to the Napa Valley community over the past decade as former president of the board of COPIA: The American Center for Wine, Food, & the Arts.

The Tychson farmhouse could not be salvaged, but Colgin and Wender have respected the identity of the historic structure. Edward Keiner of Keiner & Kasten Architects, designed the entrance facade of the new house to evoke the original, and the entry and great room fill the exact footprint of the original farmhouse's four modest rooms. It was exciting for the couple to plan a house that was totally different in feeling and scale from their Los Angeles residence. Colgin envisioned a retreat, but one with a sophisticated country tone. "Napa is a safe place," she says. "It's more rustic and agricultural than people think."

Right: The great room, built on the foundation plan of the original ranch house, showcases decorative accent pieces, such as the collection of whimsical nineteenth-century French puppets, that augment the European furnishings from the eighteenth and nineteenth centuries.

Below: The main living room displays nineteenth-century furniture pieces from Colgin's wide-ranging collection. To silence traffic noise inside the house, all windows are double-glazed.

The design evolved over time with meticulous attention to scale and detail. Keiner created a sense of spaciousness with beamed cathedral ceilings and a generous open plan that lends itself to entertaining. "The house is cozy yet open," Colgin says. "Casual dining is easy." So easy, in fact, that before the house was finished, Thomas Keller, renowned chef and owner of The French Laundry in Yountville, cooked the first Wine Auction hospitality dinner from a temporary kitchen outside and served twenty-four guests in the living room.

Colgin worked with Illya Hendrix and Tom Allardyce of Hendrix Allardyce Design in Los Angeles to create an interior that is true to the integrity of the property and the valley's history. Responding to Colgin's intention to return to the feeling that Josephine Tychson created, Hendrix Allardyce designed rooms that perfectly

Below: "Vigne" by M.P.Verneuil.

Right: In the dining room, hand-wrought ironwork decorates the doors of the wine cellar—a design by Tom Warner based on the idea of a root cellar. "The Boy" by Louis Lang, c. 1847, hangs to the left of the cellar's entrance.

absorbed the antiques—American pieces from the late nineteenth century or earlier—and Colgin's art collection. "Some people build their homes around their furniture," Colgin explains. "With us, the house came first, and the period furnishings were acquired specifically for it." Among the important pieces is the rare late eighteenth-century secretary in the great room. Outside, St. Helena landscape architect Jonathan Plant has created a complementary scheme that is also carefully attuned to a historic vision for the property.

Colgin and Wender intend to contribute their vision of history, community involvement, and fine wine for many years to come. Their life in the Napa Valley is busy and bountiful, yet it affords a casual style they find both regenerating and relaxing.

The residence of Ann Colgin and Joe Wender
Original Farmhouse, c. 1882
2000; Edward Keiner, Architect

VINEYARD COTTAGE

Vineyard Cottage, the house that Stephene McKeen and George Fullerton share in the Napa Valley, not only centers their lives in the country, but refreshes and invigorates with its informal, easy, indoor-outdoor California style. Light, bright colors that reflect the couple's enthusiasm for life suffuse every room. From the living room there is a magnificent view of the landscaped grounds and a vineyard, with the Mayacamas Mountains beyond. An inviting swimming pool flanked by two redwood pavilions designed by Fullerton anchors the setting.

Although McKeen and Fullerton lead fast-paced lives involving international travel, their energy never flags in caring for their Napa retreat. Fullerton has applied his high standards from the business world to the remodeling of this 1970s ranch house, which he purchased along with the remnants of a walnut grove. "The grove truly reflects Napa history, the period in the 1920s when English walnuts were grafted onto black walnut bases and grown commercially throughout the valley," he explains.

To create the perfect atmosphere for relaxation, reflection, and parties divine, Fullerton collaborated with master builder Thomas Edwards to transform the dark, closed-in house into an open space with light filtering into every room. Edwards tore out the low ceiling that had given the

Below: McKeen's imaginative, cheery table settings are valley-renowned and perfect for dining al fresco.

Right: Fullerton's spectacular roses grace a garden entrance.

house its "small" feeling. When rebuilt, the angles of the high-pitched roof created cathedral ceilings, whose open beams allowed skylights to be inserted between rafters. Added light from rows of clerestory windows, a multitude of French doors, and enlarged window openings heighten the sense of space.

The colorful palette, predominantly in the upholstery and drapery fabrics, complements the contemporary paintings and eclectic artwork. Interior designer Daphne Churbuck of Graham Eliot in Osterville, Massachusetts, created a refreshing bedroom décor with primary colors and crisp white accents. Her country theme has just the right touch of sophistication, bringing the feeling of a breath of clean, fresh air on a bright spring morning.

Wood shingles and an exterior gray and white color scheme reminiscent of a Cape Cod cottage reflect Fullerton's New

England roots. Napa-based garden designer Nancy Driscoll extended the house's entertainment space into the landscape and gardens. Driscoll's plans create large and small cutting gardens and a number of different areas for entertaining, including an enlarged deck, small flagstone patios, nearby BBQ and wine bar docks, and paved eating areas. Master host McKeen appreciatively describes her work as "a labor of love." With house renovation completed, Fullerton can focus on the gardens, where symmetrical beds of profuse and fragrant white Iceberg roses have matured in only two years. In the meantime, McKeen often gathers friends for festive evenings. Perfect planning of this light-hearted yet sophisticated Napa Valley cottage has created an idyllic atmosphere for both gardening and parties.

Residence of Stephene McKeen and
George Fullerton, 2000
California Ranch House

*Left and above: Interior designs by
Daphne Churbuck, of Graham Eliot in
Massachusetts, blend a traditional sensibility with a playful color palette that
heightens the effect of sunlight.*

The Napa Valley and its defining mountain ranges hold many secret passages and hidden buildings. Such a place, a modest house, originally a hunting lodge built in the 1940s for the owners of the more imposing stone residence down the hill, remains sequestered in a private woods. The comfortable sense of place and settled feeling of the home is what friends describe as "the real Napa."

Built as a retreat, the property was purchased by the current owner for the same purpose. Today, the house has become his main residence, a casual mountaintop setting that suits a new life that combines occasional trips to San Francisco with a full social calendar in the valley.

The original plan worked well as a hunting lodge. A large entry foyer linked two wings, one for the public rooms and the other for bedrooms. Today, the design still provides for easy living, with the many small bedrooms, created for a dorm situation, now perfect for houseguests. On the other side of the entry, the living room, kitchen, master bedroom suite, and music studio/office are conducive to entertaining small gatherings.

Ensconced in the foliage of the oak-filled hillside, the wood-sided house reflects its environment with a harmonious green exterior and a muted, rustically finished interior. Unfinished, unstained, floor-to-ceiling cedar paneling throughout creates a warm, low-key atmosphere. Conversational furniture groupings accented with a variety of decorative objects blends well with the rustic wall finish. Everything has personal significance, and the interiors have evolved naturally as the collections have expanded. Antiques with the glowing patina of age and care reveal the owner's sophisticated taste.

Many wood-trimmed windows make the interior a well-lit space enhanced by the accents of dark wood furniture. Private patios and landings with views of the valley bring the landscape inside. Within the angled fence of the lower front entry, garden seating areas and a winding path to a swimming pool invite visitors to linger.

Hunting Cabin, circa 1940

Preceding pages: The wooden residence built as a hunting lodge in the 1940s sports a warm green stain.

Right: A Barbara Morgan black and white photograph of Martha Graham in the late 1930s dominates the wall facing shelves that display an American Victorian clock beside a favorite small bronze sculpture by Nathan Oliveira from Charles Campbell Gallery in San Francisco. A Peter Volcas glazed pierced ceramic plate sculpture is also displayed. The grand piano delights guests by becoming a mechanized player piano.

Left: A painting immortalizing the agricultural past of America's West presides over a breakfast table, while an eclectic collection of antiques and art from all over the world fills the living room with memories and atmosphere.

Right: A portrait of the homeowner's great-great-grandparents hangs over a cluster of early-twentieth-century Dutch glazed ceramic vases from the Gouda factory. A Mexican "retablo" painting on tin shares the tabletop space of an eighteenth-century Danish chest of drawers.

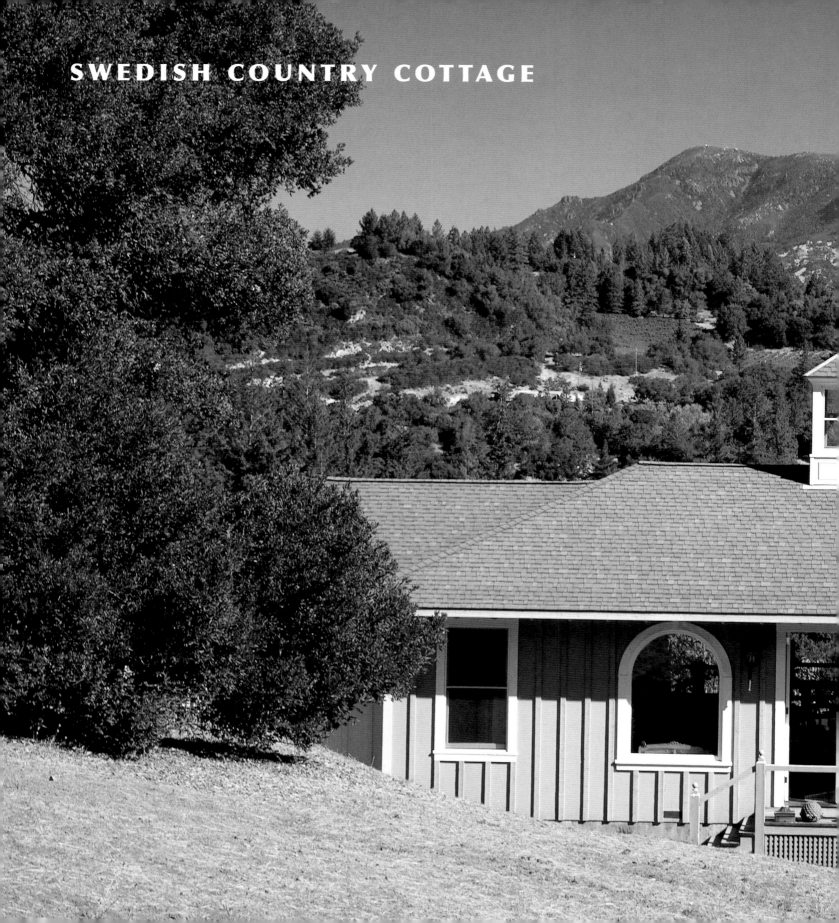

SWEDISH COUNTRY COTTAGE

Intellectually, artist Ira Yeager lives in the world of eighteenth-century France. His passion for that era permeates his entire life, including the architecture and interiors that surround him, the subjects that he paints, and the music that he listens to.

At the edge of a bucolic field and walnut grove, Yeager and architectural designer Richard Horwath built a simple barn-like cottage with a magnificent view of Mt. St. Helena. Located one ridge over from the painter's studio in Calistoga's mountains, the cottage is reminiscent of barns in the Swedish countryside. Wide arched windows and a cupola adorn the small wooden building, giving it a touch of elegance. Pairs of nine-foot tall French doors and various side windows bring sunlight during the day and filter the fading light at dusk. The exterior is painted a chalky Prussian blue, a color Yeager painstakingly blended himself. An impressive collection of eighteenth-century French, Dutch, Swedish, and English antiques fills the interior, demonstrating his love of the gracious customs and culture of the bygone era that inspires him.

For over four decades, Yeager has answered the alluring call of exotic places, letting them guide his art and his life. He has lived and painted throughout Europe and the Mediterranean, lingering in Greece, Italy, France, and Morocco. The drama and sensuality of his life's experiences fill each of his canvases and each of his homes. Now he resides in the Napa Valley, immersed in all things French of two hundred years ago. He surrounds himself with a palette of muted colors in worn, faded rugs and period furniture that he has discovered at French flea markets or in American auctions.

Yeager fearlessly juxtaposes the rural and the urban, the formal and the informal in this country setting. Festive dinner parties are held in one all-encompassing room where a full-scale German wagon with woven reed siding, an intricately painted pine armoire, early-nineteenth-century Swedish chairs upholstered in a rich creamy velvet, a rustic apple picking ladder, and gilded wood ecclesiastical candlesticks are placed with Yeager's natural sense of whimsy and impeccable eye. A few of his own colorful paintings hang on the walls. They are delightfully idiosyncratic and expressive, whether abstract, representational, historic, or a melange of these elements.

Yeager has accomplished the admirable goal of living as he chooses, honestly and unconventionally, inhabiting a singular, created world by surrounding himself with beautiful and beloved objects that clearly inspire him and bring him joy.

Residence of Ira Yeager, 1997
Richard Horwath, Architectural Designer

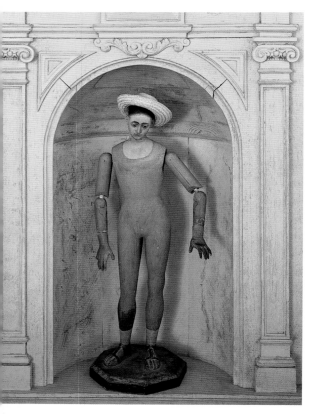

Left: A French artist's doll fills the niche of a painted country corner cupboard.

Right: Facing a farmhouse wagon is a painted country armoire and a stag and child painting by homeowner and artist Ira Yeager. Gilt and gesso ecclesiastical candlesticks complement the clean pure lines of the nineteenth-century Swedish dining chairs.

Following pages: The scene of the living room's authentic eighteenth-century furnishings transports guests to a gentler era. A game table with ivory and woodchip pieces of a "whist" set, a carved wooden pedestal with wig and cockaded tri-corn hat, a fabric screen with eighteenth-century French gentlemen's coats and a book press are among the evocative mix of urban and country furnishings. A simple profile in pastel that is set on the mantle was done by Yeager in 1999 on a trip to Zacatecas.

Preceding pages: The rammed earth house of David Easton and Cynthia Wright was designed with the proportions and detailing of an authentic French farmhouse.

Right: Drought-tolerant and native plantings of California thrive in this Mediterranean-inspired landscape.

David Easton and his wife, Cynthia Wright, chose four acres of flatland abutting a valley vineyard as the ideal site for their new home. It is a naturally wooded area near the picturesque, oak-studded foothills of the lower Napa Valley's eastern border. Inspired by their European travels, Easton, an author and engineer, and Wright, a photographer, designed their house as a French farmhouse. To build it, they chose rammed earth construction, an unconventional but ecologically sound method in which Easton has substantial expertise.

Steeped in California sensibility, drought tolerant plantings and flowering plants evocative of Mediterranean gardens spill over walls and terra cotta pots, burst with growth along fine gravel paths, and form a lush border for the pool, while a thick grapevine covers the main patio arbor. The scene evokes the countryside of southern France.

The couple's research and close observation in France are evident in the house, where the design, proportions, and detailing create an authenticity often missing in contemporary interpretations of the vernacular. For Easton and Wright, it was essential to travel and study the buildings to understand what makes the architecture authentic. They were determined that the house would have "the purity and strength of thick, sturdy walls, the weight of hefty wrought iron details, and earthy rich

Preceding pages: Thick walls and the elimination of unnecessary detailing create a simplicity and clarity of design that is viscerally pleasing.

Below: Bold, colorful accents of pottery, flowers, and book bindings are reinforced by the warm, planar stucco wall surfaces.

Right: Natural materials and proportionally large furnishings are used throughout the serene bathroom design.

Residence of David Easton and Cynthia Wright, 1999
Michael Baushke, Architect
David Easton and Cynthia Wright, Architectural Designers

accents in interiors that were based on muted relaxed tones." Rammed earth construction was ideal for these goals. "With it, the materials speak for themselves," says Easton. Rammed earth constructrion, though over 4000 years old, is considered the "new adobe." Packed, dried earth was used by many of the indigenous peoples of America to build shelters. In the past twenty years, rammed earth has reemerged as one of the most economical, ecologically responsible, and quality means of construction.

The couple loves the effect of sunlight within the house and the indescribable calm that comes from the solidity of the forms. For them, it is not so much about history—they are not trying to go back in time—as it is about a sense of place. They define that sense and that place as an agrarian compound. These aesthetic concerns coexist happily with the benefits of rammed earth construction, which include energy efficiency, air quality, longevity, durability, low maintenance, safety, fire resistance, and moderate construction cost.

Easton and Wright are committed to affordable housing and openly share their knowledge. Current efforts involve a rammed earth facility for farm workers in the Napa Valley and construction workshops leading to building a manufacturing facility in Africa.

ITALIANATE FARMHOUSE

*Preceding pages: The Italianate farm-
house of Erika and Austin Hills appears
as if nestled in the hills of Tuscany.*

*Right: A flurry of colorful wildflowers
cheers the main entrance to the
Hillses' country estate.*

Austin and Erika Hills have captured
the romance of life in their sunlit
hilltop country house, framed as it
might be in Italy by one thousand acres of
vineyards and the rocky peak of a nearby
mountain. An olive grove and kitchen
garden gently cascade down the backyard
slope while hundreds of lavender plants fill
a side yard, and, close to the house, an
abundance of wildflowers move with the
breezes. The beauty of this Italianate
farmhouse lies in the simplicity of its
design and an ageless quality that affirms
its European heritage. Inside, Erika Hills's
vibrant natural flair and spirited design style
contribute bold strokes of drama and color.
The rooms burst with imagination,
resplendent by day and dreamlike in the
candlelit dusk. A powerful sense of life
permeates the California household with
energy, creativity, and European warmth.

The talented team who guided the design
included two architects, the Italian Dante
Dini and Jorges de Quesada of San
Francisco, and interior designer Diane Burns
of New York. Their collaboration with the
Hillses created a striking, simple form faced
in stucco with a roof of antique tiles from
Provence. The plan is equally simple,
conceived as a series of open spaces oriented
to take advantage of light and views.

The centerpiece of the house is the
magnificent living room, a lavishly painted
eighteenth-century room from the Tyrol in

Below and right: The villa is surrounded by a thousand acres of vineyards and the picturesque foothills of the Napa Valley. Al fresco dining affords views of the bucolic countryside.

Following pages: Southern exposure to the estate provides a bright interior and nourishing sunlight for the nearby olive grove and kitchen vegetable garden.

Pages 126–127: The foyer entry is a glamorous introduction to the dramatic interiors of the Hillses' villa. Because of its extra high ceiling and rustic wood beams, the space resembles an early California mission nave.

Residence of Austin and Erika Hills, 1999
Dante Dini, Architect
Jorge de Quesada, Architect

Austria. Once a period room at the M. H. de Young Memorial Museum in San Francisco, the Tyrolean room was acquired by the Hillses at auction. The Austrian masterpiece is now twice its original size. Napa artist Evelyn Wander expertly replicated the decorative painted rococo screens, which are now complemented by a parquet floor from a French chateau of the same period. In the entry hall/reception room, designed as an ode to California missions, the exposed beam ceiling is enhanced with a shimmering mirror installation by Austrian artist Gustav Troger.

Austin, a San Franciscan who is the business partner of the successful Grgich Hills Winery, and Austrian-born Erika, an enthusiastic international art patron, have cultivated a rich life in the Napa Valley, centered around the simple pleasures of bringing people together in their home. International artists are regular houseguests, enjoying the company of local creative spirits and close friends. Of equal importance, the Hillses invite non-profit organizations to hold exceptional evening events in their grand Tyrolean room. A ballet performance by candlelight entranced an audience of sixty seated on pillows. On other evenings, the massive carved pocket doors have opened to extend the space into the adjacent entry hall for a large reception or dinner party. Whether inside the house or on the grounds, guests revel in the pleasures of country life in an atmosphere of conviviality and ease that only true romantics can create.

Above: A view through the intermediate hall from the kitchen to entry foyer features the bold use of crimson silk taffeta and gold gilt statuary for sensual drama.

Right: The Tyrolean room, a period room from the De Young Museum acquired at auction, is the magnificent centerpiece of the house. The antique European furnishings and silk upholstery complement the delicately painted panels of the eighteenth-century artwork.

Erika's gift for great style includes combining whimsical and unexpected pieces with surprising color juxtapositions that create a grand dramatic effect. In the kitchen, also used as the dining room for large gatherings, a hearth with antiqued stenciling, an open-beamed ceiling, a European farm table of wood, custom-made cabinets and counter, and the massive 125-candle centerpiece (once a sugar mold) create warmth in the sunny room.

VILLA CA' TOGA

Preceding pages: The front façade of the Palladian-style villa created by artist and muralist Carlo Marchiori presents itself as a grand theatrical stage.

Above and right: Marchiori's five-acre landscape is filled with his hand-made ruins that give the illusion of an archaeological dig in progress and immediately age the property.

For an Italian to say that he would rather live in the Napa Valley than in Italy is a tribute that suggests that this is a place where dreams come true and life is good. Venetian-born Carlo Marchiori leads such a life. Happiest when working, this classically trained artist has transformed an abandoned five-acre parcel of land near Calistoga into a fantasy estate. His faux-eighteenth-century Venetian villa, surrounded by landscape punctuated with hand-made art representing follies and ancient ruins, presents a captivating and magical world of illusion, Marchiori's canvas for expression over the past fifteen years.

Marchiori was formally trained at the Instituto Pietro Selvatico in Padua. He left

Above: Proper scale and proportion in Marchiori's murals show his mastery of design.

Right: Every inch of the master bedroom and its anteroom are painted to transport the dweller to another time and place.

Italy at 18 and has lived in such places as Japan, Canada, and Brazil, and worked as a commercial artist, cartoonist, magazine illustrator, and film animator, garnering an Academy Award nomination for his short piece, *The Drag*. He moved to the Napa Valley for a life of creating art for art's sake in the all-important sunny climate. Since then, the estate that he shares with his partner Tony Banthutham has become the center of his work.

The stage-set-like Palladian-style villa was inspired by the Villa Barbaso at Maser. Its rooms allow Marchiori to travel back in time to the eighteenth-century and beyond for inspiration and demonstrate his virtuosity as a painter on a grand scale. The flair and élan of his self-described "improvisa-

SPERATE
MISERI

The parlor at the house's entrance is Pompeiian in character.

tional, not-too-careful style" comes about, he explains, "by eye-balled estimates and sketches." His highly developed design sense ensures that his murals are in scale with volume and space. Trompe l'oeil renderings present illusions of sculpture, vignettes of historic moments, or interpretations of imagined rooms in Herculaneum or Pompeii. They resemble frescoes but are actually painted with house paint on canvas. Decorative glazed tiles are painted with representations of farcical scenes with costumed pulcinella from the commedia dell'arte. In his villa rooms, Marchiori has produced a unique atmosphere, full of imagination, wonder, and humor in a style he calls romantic sentimentalism.

On the grounds, Marchiori has extended the spirit of the villa into the landscape. To integrate the building within its setting (and as an excuse for a no-maintenance yard), Marchiori has created gardens that appear abandoned, with interpretations of ancient architectural "ruins" executed in weathered and battered stone, cement, fiberglass, and tile. Cast stone plaques, miniature architectural forms, and decorative ceramics are visual accents in the imperfect but picturesque landscape. Marchiori and a crew of assistants built a number of berms of earth and scavenged construction rubble. These now-grass-covered mounds and groves of mature trees planted a decade ago give the estate a time-worn, natural appearance. In fact, this "pleasurable creative achievement" is entirely the work of Carlo Marchiori.

House tours are given regularly, May–October.

Residence of Carlo Marchiori and
Tony Banthutham, 1988
Paul Bonacci and Lucy Schlaffer, Architects

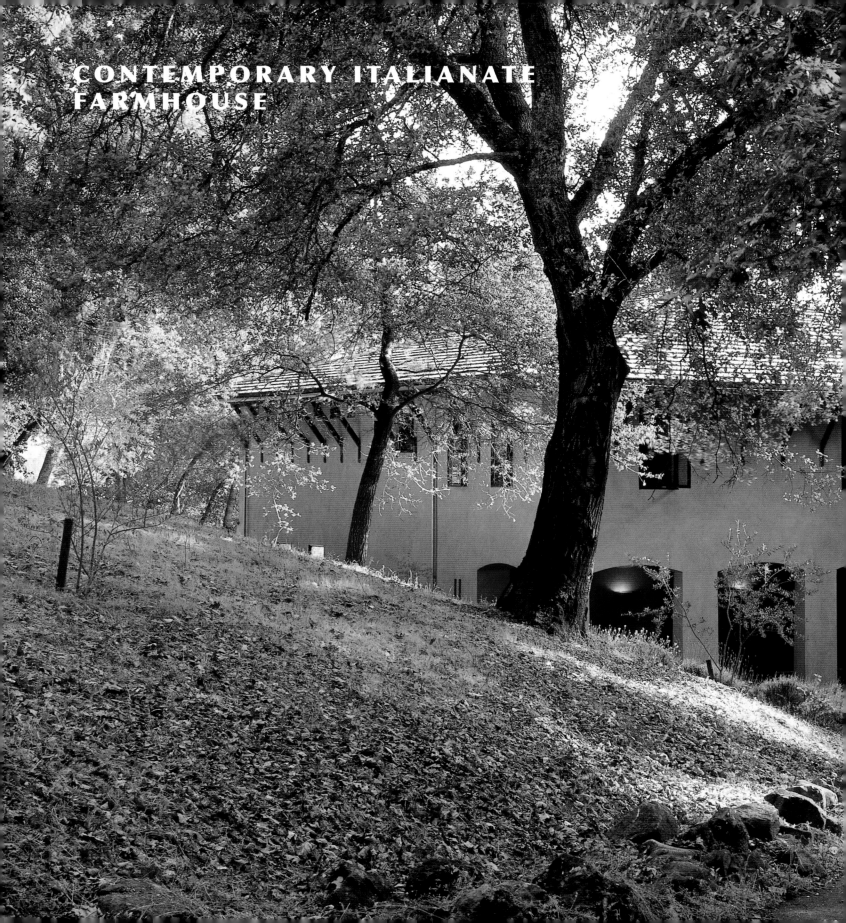

CONTEMPORARY ITALIANATE
FARMHOUSE

Right: Groin vaulting and thick stucco piers accent the deep space of the main entrance giving it a historical reference.

Following pages: Repeated forms alluding to historic Italian architectural elements include a row of small clerestory windows and walls punctuated with divided windows that resemble monolithic doors.

It all began when James Konrad took a vacation from his post-graduate studies in nuclear medicine to explore the Napa Valley. En route to the Mayacamas Winery, he was intrigued by a "for sale" sign that led him further up the mountain. At the site he met Edmond Maudiere from Epernay, France, a thirteenth-generation winemaker and retired *chef de cave* of Moet-Hennessy, and John Wright, founding president of Domaine Chandon. The next thing he knew, he had bought sixty acres of dirt—on a handshake.

Viticulturalists James and Leslie Konrad now grow Cabernet Sauvignon and Malbec grapes on the rolling slopes of the property in the Mt. Veeder Appellation. In 1989 the couple decided to move to the Napa Valley to be closer to the vineyard and purchased land near St. Helena. A trip to the romantic villages of the Veneto suggested the style for their new house. To educate herself about the architectural design process, Leslie attended a series of discussions among architects and designers organized by Andrew Batey, a Cambridge-educated architect now based in Napa Valley. She found the ideas exchanged fascinating and helpful in the defining the issues surrounding the selection of an architect.

The Konrads wanted to build responsibly, respecting the land, and knew they wanted to work with an architect who shared their

Below and Right: Colorful furnishings and the Konrad's artwork accent the spacious living room.

concerns and understood the vernacular style of Italian farmhouses. The couple selected Ned Forrest of Forrest Architects, and they could not be more enthusiastic about their choice. "Ned strives for timelessness, though his designs borrow elements from the past, like the strength of Tuscan forms," Leslie says. "We made the right team with the right vision."

The house, completed in 1990, is still a new and fresh design. Forrest's work is intentionally sculptural and objective, but it projects a strong historical perspective. Modernist sensibilities are informed by a love and knowledge of Italy and its rich architectural heritage. The house is carefully sited within a private wood of old growth oaks on a hillside that allows valley views. The configuration of the plan, the proportions of the rooms, and the details all contribute to a strong sense of place. The plan centers on a great room that is both spacious and open to other rooms, creating a perfect setting for informal entertaining and displaying the couple's art collection. Details like the band of small clerestory windows below the cathedral ceiling show imagination in combining the contemporary and the traditional. While whispering the past through reinterpreted Old World forms, the design of the entire house embodies the present.

Residence of James and Leslie Konrad, 1990
Ned Forrest, Architect

REDWOOD HOUSE

Below: Moroccan textiles imported by designer Carol Romano add richness and warmth to the living room's various sitting areas.

Right: Shannon's informal garden, integrating the gigantic California Redwood, complements the design and atmosphere of the Craftsman Bungalow and provides a comfortable outdoor habitat.

Shannon Kuleto's "in town" house, shared with her son, Daniel, is a Craftsman bungalow, built about 1910, with a massive California redwood in the front yard. Known as Redwood House, it is a fine example of the residential architecture inspired by the Arts and Crafts movement, which was influential in America in the early twentieth century. The Arts and Crafts ideal, that art and life should harmonize in the home, is embraced by Kuleto, a food and wine historian.

The modest house incorporates architectural features and finishes typical of the best craftsman principles. Developed in reaction to early-twentieth-century industrialization and mechanization, the bungalow was built of natural materials, predominantly stone and wood, and emphasized the workmanship and craft of design. The form derives from the *bengalas* of India, primitive, one-story huts that featured low, sweeping lines and wide verandahs. The term was popularized and transliterated by British officers in the nineteenth century and applied to rural American farmhouses and small English cottages.

The defining feature of the exterior was the front porch. Its design included a low-pitched gable or hip roof with a prominent over-hang, often supported by heavy, projecting rafters. The welcoming porch became a bridge between the casual design of natural plantings in the front yard and

Below: One of many Craftsman-style details found throughout the house is this iron wall sconce.

Right: The predominant theme of warm red is carried throughout the house's interiors in glass candleholders, leather upholstery, hand-woven rugs, and textile throws.

Following pages: Shannon's collection of red glassware and an abundance of candlelight are perfect accents for the dark-stained wood of the period furnishings and the many built-in features of the house.

the house's main entrance. The porch also encouraged the indoor-outdoor living style and closeness to nature promoted by Arts and Crafts ideals and so important to Californians today.

On the Redwood House porch, rugs are scattered, cushions are abundant, and twig and willow furnishings, padded and draped with comfortable lap blankets, shawls, and other necessities in true nineteenth-century fashion create an extended, intimate living room, perfect for star-gazing or sipping early morning coffee. The porch overlooks an abundant display of historically appropriate cutting flowers, herbs, and shade plantings.

Inside, firelight, dark-stained clear heart redwood trim, and unusual ruby-red glass accents create a warm, enveloping atmosphere. Kuleto has used a Craftsman-inspired palette of earthy, warm browns, beiges, and variations on terra cotta, with striking jewel-toned accents built on a theme of passionate red, for furniture, leather upholstery, hand-woven rugs and pillow-covers. A backdrop of butter cream-colored walls sets off the myriad decorative objects, fabric textures, and detailed forms that fill the house and keep it lively. With this scheme, Kuleto achieves one of the most significant goals of the Arts and Crafts movement: the creation of environments to support the confluence of art, nature, and spirit, where the individual artistic expression is respected and celebrated.

CALIFORNIA CRAFTSMAN BUNGALOW

Fresh white paint and new light sources have updated and brightened this California bungalow near the historic downtown of St. Helena. The intimacy and charm of the cottage, built about 1910, has allowed Jerry Dark and interior designer Monty Collins to make a surprisingly pleasant transition from the isolation of country life to small town sociability, where neighbors feel free to drop by their comfortable home.

Collins and Dark maintained the character of the Arts and Crafts-style structure and its easy interior flow by enhancing its light with naturally reflective white paint and strategically placed skylights. Sturdy and solid, bungalows have simple lines and minimal detailing, that create a restrained, calm atmosphere and a surprisingly contemporary image. The Collins Dark house has a chameleon quality that integrates its original architecture identity with an eclectic mix of contemporary art, sculpture, and furniture.

The all-white setting feels right for the art and objects the couple have acquired through the years, but the installation is carefully orchestrated. Collins, whose firm has offices in San Francisco and Seattle, applied his professional principles to the design. He advises clients to think about continuity and to edit collections according to that vision. "This house is all about editing," he says. "Houses need continuity."

As a Southerner who grew up in Mobile, Alabama, surrounded by great old collections, he admits it's a challenge.
In this house, the walls and floors recede, becoming background. The furnishings and accessories, the colors and fabrics give the rooms their distinct personalities. "Often there are no outstanding architectural details in a room, but it does matter," he explains. "The profile of a chair can be quite remarkable."

As a favor from one southern gentleman to another, Georgia-born landscape designer Brandon Tyson created the garden. Recognizing that the house deserved a special design, he turned the small outdoor space into a series of intimate garden rooms. There are five separate but confluent entertainment areas, woven together with decking, patios, paved and planted areas, and water elements. The spaces include a linear side deck, a swimming pool with a private lounging lawn area, and a back deck and hot tub surrounded by lush, exotic plantings. Transitional paths are paved with Chinese granite or New York cobblestone, and an intriguing axial route, framed by a high side fence, leads from the front gate to the studio in the rear. The space now appears larger than it is, and all of it can be used, thanks to the exceptional planning and planting scheme.

Residence of Monty Collins and Jerry Dark, c. 1910
California Craftsman Bungalow, c. 1910

Preceding pages: Window openings, heavy moldings, and the abundant vertical and horizontal elements in the Craftsman design are accentuated by the exterior's all-white palette. Interior designer and homeowner Monty Collins continues the same palette inside.

Right: An axial plan that includes a paved route from the front gate to the rear studio enlarges the outdoor entertainment space. Lush plantings, a side deck, and a Jacuzzi, all in the masterful plan by landscape designer Brandon Tyson, fill the small backyard with useful spaces.

Right: A "Joyful Buddha" oversees the den where an early-nineteenth-century French armchair retains its original leather upholstery and a pair of upholstered chairs made by Pessin Fournir add comfort. Garden trellis ornaments decorate the mantle on either side of a c. 1870 footed glass bowl.

Above: A soothing palette of white on white is the best backdrop for the brass bead crystal chandelier by Light Opera designer Jim Mizner. The concrete table is by Michael Taylor and the nineteenth-century French chairs are covered in a Fortuny print.

Left: The gold gilt chair is an eighteenth-century reproduction by J. Robert Scott, covered in a contemporary Scalamandre fabric. Patinaed architectural mirrors that Collins found at Petera in New York lean into the corners of the room, while a coffee table made of a slab of Selenite mined in Utah adds layered dimension just feet away from a hand-crafted stick table from Georgia. The antique lamp is crackleware.

Right: Clerestory windows and skylights make the master bath bright. Colorful artwork punctuates the all-white surfaces.

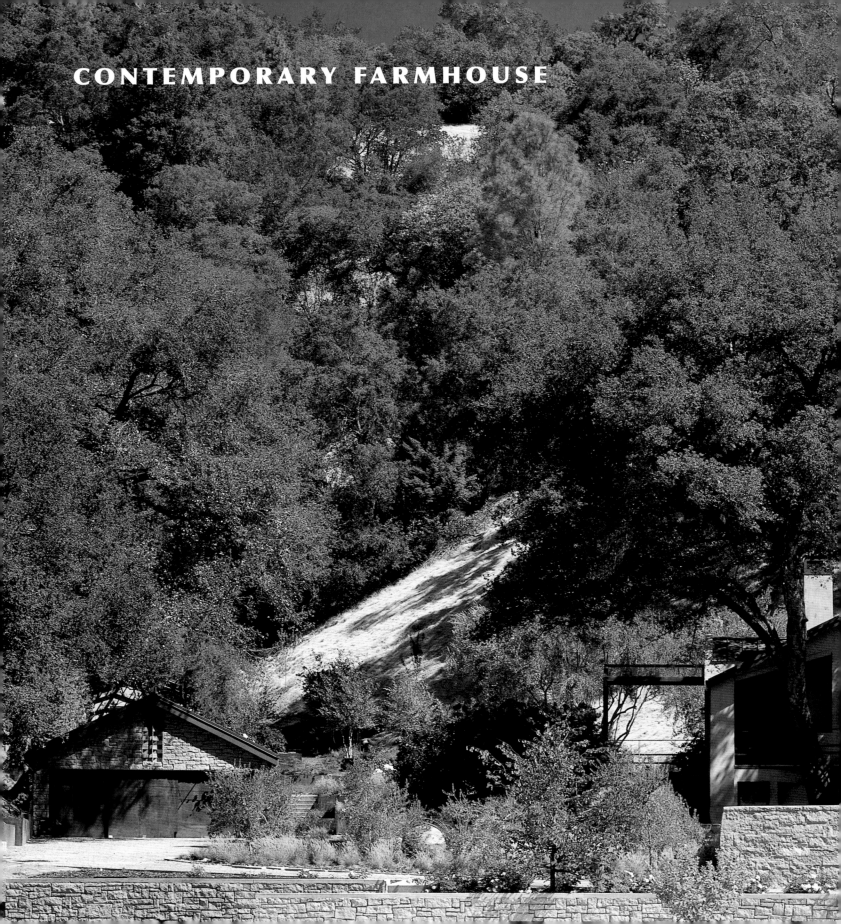

CONTEMPORARY FARMHOUSE

Preceding pages: Landscape Architect Jack Chandler designed his contemporary house in stucco and steel, using earth-born colors and textures to complement the California native plants in the landscape plan and the indigenous flora of the mountain setting.

Left top: A metal trellis, limestone BBQ, and paved patio overlook the lap pool and a side garden where natural stone spheres rest among California native plantings.

Left bottom: The dining room's centerpiece is a single-board custom table that seats twelve, surrounded by contemporary Italian chairs.

Right: Chandler combines the artistry of metal sculpture with landscape design at the main entrance by using plates of rusted, heavy-gauge steel the color of iron ore for sturdy retaining walls and augmenting the wood and stucco house with structural and decorative steel beams.

When award-winning metal sculptor and landscape architect Jack Chandler designed this house and its gardens for himself and his wife, Michelle Amendola, his holistic approach reflected the skills he has honed over the past twenty years in professional practice. For Chandler, understanding and integrating the elements of air, water, and earth are the keys to creating a pleasing, simple, and elegant formal environment. The main house, set on a wooded hillside north of Calistoga, is an unpretentious contemporary form with a nod to the Italian farmhouse. Earthy materials—rusted metal, warm-toned stucco, and Napa stone—complement the natural setting. The building meanders up the hill, a seemingly small structure that actually encloses a generous open floor plan with windows oriented for natural light. In all aspects, the house can be seen as a sculpture

Left: In the dining room, the rusty pati-na of the keys in Chandler's creation of "found art" complements the warm tones in the simple oak bureau below.

Right: Sheet metal chemically treated by Chandler serves as a dynamic fireplace over-mantel and artwork. Over-sized ceramic floor tiles set at a diagonal and a luscious red textile chair covering add flair to the interior design.

of metal and stucco that serves as a center-piece for the informal grounds as well as a voluminous container for the art and furnishings within.

Chandler, principal of Jack Chandler and Associates in Yountville, uses as light a touch here as he does in many of his other Western projects. He prefers gardens that are untamed, using native grasses and herbaceous plantings such as lavender and rosemary as well as many drought-tolerant plants that appear to be naturally placed. Color, fragrance, and the sound of water are common to all his designs, conveying tranquility and infinity.

Terraced planting areas are enclosed by walls and stairs made of striking materials. On the back hill, a stairway with packed sand treads has risers made of sheet metal weathered to the color of burnt earth. On either side, larger pieces of heavy gauge steel, rusted to the same deep tone, serve as retaining walls. The path that leads guests through the multi-leveled gardens reaches a broad patio at the summit. Its rustic pergola of thin hand-hewn logs is visible from below. Elsewhere, low, stone retaining walls bear the weight of a glistening lap pool and orient the driveway toward a rustic rock garage faced with mighty steel doors rusted to earthy brown.

Below: Well-placed antiques and found pieces such as the ocean liner smoke stack are colorful and whimsical focal points placed against the muted walls painted with a mixture of gray-green and ochre.

Right: From the mezzanine balcony, the dining and living rooms are seen as a continuous, open space with an extensive ceiling height and walls of windows that add to the expansiveness.

Following pages: Loar's contemporary farmhouse, built on a hilltop, affords views of the valley below.

Architectural features of the main house include weathered steel beams that give the entry porch roof a unique profile and an intricate pergola that integrates house and gardens through materials and color. Inside, walls painted a complex blend of green, light ochre, and gray let the colors and textures of the metal art, fine stone and wood surfaces, and various textiles take precedence. This home celebrates the passion that Chandler and his wife have for the art of sculpture in its many and varied forms, including interpretations in architecture and landscape as well as unconventional and masterful metal design, wood and glass objects, and custom-designed furnishings.

*Residence of Jack Chandler and
Michelle Amendola, 2002
Jack Chandler, Architectural Designer*

CALIFORNIA CONTEMPORARY

In the living room, bumped-out spaces designed for Loar's large pieces of furniture, such as the late-eighteenth-century French armoire, allow for more floor space and create a more expansive feeling. The large farm table is constructed of eighteenth-century French floorboards. Early-nineteenth-century Italian heraldic floor candelabras flank the fireplace. The ceiling height and room dimensions were carefully proportioned for the often over-sized furnishings.

As director of COPIA: The American Center for Wine, Food, & the Arts in Napa, Peggy Loar works in a sleek, contemporary office designed by the Polshek Partnership. At home, she wanted warm country design that could absorb and display an eclectic group of furniture and decorative objects. Her home is filled with found treasures, largely collected during a decade of international travel when she was director of SITES (Smithsonian Institution Traveling Exhibition Services). This sophisticated mix of furnishings, soft and comfortable or carved and ornate, contrasts dramatically with her work environment, and that's just what she wants.

The house appears to crawl up the ridge of a hill at the rustic end of Brown's Valley. Only one room deep, the plan orients each of the multi-level spaces toward bucolic views and provides the rooms with hours of natural light. Loar designed the house herself, consulting with Sausalito architect Allan Nichol, Miami designer Kevin Crain, and interior designer Cheryl Brantner of Los Angeles. The interior design revolves around the Loar's furniture, with high ceilings and deep niches to accommodate overscaled pieces. A tall, barrel vaulted ceiling in the dining room lends a monastic flavor to the room, which contains a massive French linen press.

Below: A monastic sense pervades the dining room with its barrel-vaulted ceiling, a 13-foot solid plank French farm table, and high-backed chairs whose covers change with the seasons (here, Butterscotch brushed linen). At the far end of the room a c.1898 Italian art nouveau "stile floreale" floor lamp with blown glass shade adds verticality to the long, narrow room.

Right: Lighting designer Susan Huey and Interior Designer Cheryl Brantner of Los Angeles, who also designed Julia's Kitchen at COPIA, gave Loar's kitchen style and ambiance, adding punch with black accents such as the granite countertops and wrought-iron lighting fixtures. Double-tiered cabinets add sophistication as well as extra storage space. A lead garden ornament in the form of a seed pod holds olive branches from the property's grove.

Loar originally intended to build the house of rammed earth or hay bales because she liked the heavy interior feeling and the rustic wall surfaces. The change to wood beam construction retained the thick walls she envisioned, and allowed them to be cut back so that large pieces, such as armoires, could be inset flush with the wall on either side, saving floor space. The warm feeling Loar sought for the interior was also achieved. Walls finished with textured plaster and painted a mild ochre color not only produced a warm tone, but the process was less expensive and crack proof. Unobtrusive contemporary lighting designed by Susan Huey also created a more spacious feeling.

The house was also built for entertaining, with an emphasis on food preparation (often by a famous chef) and an enjoyable dining experience. Loar jokes about positioning the kitchen a step above the dining room. "Here in the valley," she says, "the origins of the supper, the kitchen and the chef, are celebrated, while the diners enjoy the whole process as an audience."

Below: In the main bathroom, a stylized Athenian drape of transparent gauze was designed by Loar, then custom sewn. A wooden carved Nandi from a sixteenth-century Indian temple hangs between a pair of black and gold gilt framed mirrors that recall the Renaissance. An art historian, Loar enjoys juxtaposing objects from different cultures and times to stimulate the senses.

Right: Carved wood doors from Peru close off the main bedroom. A nineteenth-century neo-Baroque Guatemalan tabernacle is placed in the sunken architectural niche over the head of the bed, replacing a more traditional headboard. The bed is dressed in lavender and taupe burnt silk velvet. A fresh water fish spear is an unusual and interesting decorative accent.

Although Loar has never worked with an interior designer, her expert eye, her incredible visual memory, and her ability to make quick decisions have served her well. She never looks for a specific item. "Furnishings and style just happen," she says. Now antique wooden furnishings, luxurious fabrics, found doors and windows, stone surfaces, and muted colors all blend well in the voluminous space in a style she calls "modern medieval." This country retreat embraces the past and a myriad of memories for its cosmopolitan owner.

Residence of Peggy A. Loar, 1999
Alan Nichol, Architect
Peggy Loar, Architectural Designer
Kevin Crain, Designer
Cheryl Brantner, Designer

CLOS PEGASE WINERY RESIDENCE

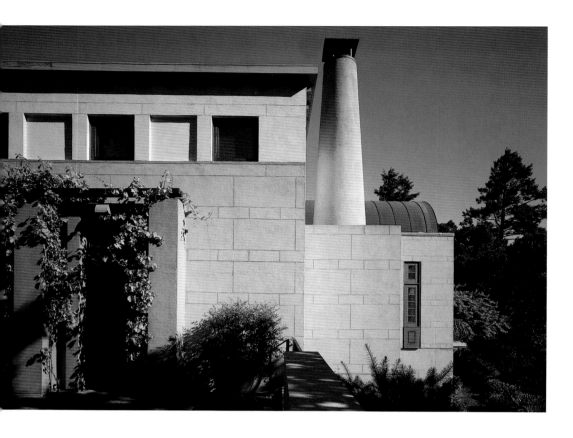

Preceding pages: The Clos Pegase Winery Residence designed by Michael Graves, 1987.

Left: Graves's post-modern architecture recalls classical forms.

Right: A view of the nearby foothills and a lush green lawn augment the straight lines and forms of Graves's outdoor hardscape for the compound.

It has been almost two decades since Jan Shrem and his wife, Mitsuko, decided to leave France and move to California with their two children. The couple first lived in Mitsuko's native Japan, where Jan Shrem owned a successful publishing firm. After 25 years in Japan and as a publisher and an art collector, Shrem decided, as he says, "to live actively" in his two great passions, wine and art.

To that end, Shrem studied enology for three years at the University of Bordeaux. He soon met legendary winemaker André Tchelistcheff, who became his consultant in California. The Napa Valley seemed ideal for his home and business and, because of its proximity to the San Francisco Museum of Modern Art, for his collecting interests as well. Producing fine wines and living nearby, as French winery owners traditionally do, in a setting where he could display his extensive collection of modern art and sculpture was Jan Shrem's vision of paradise.

In 1984 the San Francisco Museum of Art sponsored a design competition that proposed a creative collaboration between architects and artists to combine fine art and a commercial project. Clos Pegase Winery and Residence is based on the winning scheme by Michael Graves and artist Edward Schmidt. The complex in Calistoga comprises fifty acres of vineyards in front of the winery, which is set deep in the distance with the residence hidden among native oaks on the hillock beyond.

Painted in an evocative duo of terra cotta tones, the private villa rests gently on the hilltop, presenting a contemporary interpretation of classical architecture in a

Eighteenth-century Venetian furniture, upholstered in vivid royal blue velvet and white glazed pavers of Mt. Vesuvius clay with an under-coat of blue dramatically pull the colors from Shrem's outstanding collection of modern art. In the sitting room, a carpet from the Forbidden City rests below an Alexander Calder mobile. The entrance is flanked on the left by a 1937 Yves Tanguy scape with a De Kooning bronze below, and on the right by a figure by Francis Picabia, 1923.

Tuscan-like landscape. Sited toward the south for maximum exposure to the sunlight, the house is laid out on a formal axis established by an entry corridor that includes a barrel-vaulted rotunda and proceeds like an ecclesiastical nave. Living pavilions on either side of the central axis include, among a larger number of rooms, a glazed garden conservatory with views of the nearby mountains, a color-filled living room that serves as a gallery for the Shrems' art collection, and a small, serene reflection room in Japanese motif. The house is a sleek piece of contemporary sculpture built with the highest level of craftsmanship. Exquisite detailing features Honduran mahogany doors, woodwork, and inlaid patterned floors. The feeling is smooth, simple, and chic, perfectly attuned to the couple's aesthetic sensibilities.

The grounds include multiple levels of sculpture gardens, a pool, and various reception and entertainment terraces contained in hardscape that links them to the house. Although the Shrems enjoy regular visits to New York, it is in the Napa Valley that their life plan has been fulfilled. The pleasures of daily life have come to include creating in a ceramic studio for her and a brisk walk to work down the winding drive for him.

Residence of Jan and Mitsuko Shrem, 1987
Michael Graves, Architect

Left: The dining room's floor of inlaid hardwoods complements the large table made in the Napa Valley. On the right-side wall, a painting by Mata hangs above a grouping of Korean chests, and on either side, matching Italian Baroque tapestries hold scenes depicting grapes and vines. The pair of wood and gilt pedestals are nineteenth-century French.

Above: In the front hallway with its small rotunda, the main axis of the house creates a pleasing formality and guides the eye toward a distant focal point. Impeccable detailing in oak and cherry fills the interiors, with doors and window framing in Honduras mahogany.

185

MINIMALIST RESIDENCE

Above: Newquist designed gardens comprised of blocked-out areas of tightly planted herbs and flowers that form highly textural solid masses.

Right: The landscape plan of grasses, herbs, and colorful flowers provides a natural and serene setting for the simple sculptural buildings of Newquist's house and garage.

Five years ago, art patron Louise Newquist sold her house in Southern California and its outdoor sculpture she had collected with her late husband, Richard, and moved to the Napa Valley. The new house she built on two acres of the valley floor was conceived primarily to accommodate her collection of minimalist art but also to reflect the serenity of the area. Designed with architect Marcus Springer, the structure is itself minimalist art, composed of corrugated metal box forms appropriately set in a subdued, drought-tolerant landscape. Inside, vast, open rooms hold panels of colorful art that awaken the senses like a splash of fresh, cold water.

Newquist cites the late minimalist artist Donald Judd's work as the inspiration for the structure in both form and materials. Judd used industrial materials such as metal and plywood to create sleek sculptures, or, as he preferred to call them, "unarticulated objects in space," that he believed had

Black leather sofas by Le Corbusier form the conversation area in the living room. The far wall holds "Triptich," acrylic on canvas, by John Miller. "Ka-Who-So," John McCracken's polyester resin plank rests against the wall, while an etched glass piece, "Untitled Window," by Michael Heizer serves as a room divider. "Light Trap" by Ron Cooper in green polyethylene resin overlooks the anodized aluminum breakfast table designed by Newquist and four Toleto chairs by Spanish designer Jorge Pensi.

strong formal lives of their own. Newquist agrees, adding, "Raw materials are delicious. They have great color and texture."

The main residence is a fifty-eight foot square. The interiors were planned around Newquist's large pieces with windows and skylights inserted into the walls and roof to light the space. To moderate the variable temperatures, Ronald Cox of the Napa Construction Company installed heat-deflecting elastomeric material on the roof and insulated the plywood and corrugated metal walls.

Newquist is learning to live in a voluminous space where rooms are not traditionally defined and large works of art might serve as a dividers. White walls and a cement floor allow the color in the art to take precedence. For Newquist, this is all-important because her response to art has always been visceral and emotional rather than cerebral. Although she may know the artists, she focuses on the work. "Art is not about the artist," she says. "It all starts from the piece."

The versatile interior space lends itself to entertaining as well. A thirty-year patron of the arts, Newquist often opens the house to not-for-profit organizations, hosting receptions for COPIA: The American Center for Wine, Food, & the Arts and luncheons for the di Rosa Preserve, a foundation and site in Napa County with an arts and environmental conservation mission, of which she is a director.

Above: The focal point of the entry to the library/office is De Wain Valentine's "Lavender Column," 1968, in cast polyester resin.

Right: Ron Davis's three acrylic on canvas pieces that seem to float over the oven create dynamic movement in the kitchen, while Peter Liashkov's "Second White Arch," 1980, a glass construction, dominates the side wall. An Eskimo sculpture in whale bone rests on the countertop.

Following pages: The entrance gallery and dining room is often used for receptions and parties for non-profit organizations such as COPIA: The American Center for Wine, Food, & the Arts and the di Rosa Preserve. Among its outstanding wall-mounted pieces are Craig Kauffman's untitled acrylic lacquer on plexiglass, the focal point of the far wall, and James Hayward's "Suite in Five Pieces #11," oil and wax on canvas on board.

The grounds were conceived as art in exterior space. As a result of Newquist's sophisticated design sense, the rear and side gardens are studies in subtlety, containing low, square beds of tightly planted herbs that read as solid, textural masses. In the front yard, a barely perceptible path meanders through gently swaying grasses and lavender. Although these gardens have different plantings, each blends with the house's design, its color, and its textures. The visual impact of the whole is a sensual, soothing work of art.

Residence of Louise Newquist, 1999
Marcus Springer, Architect
Louise Newquist, Architectural Designer

CASA CABERNET

A mutual love of contemporary art led to Angus and Margaret Wurtele's meeting at the Walker Art Center in Minneapolis. After their marriage, the Wurteles continued to live in Minneapolis, where Angus was the CEO of a successful corporation. At the same time, Angus dreamed of owning a winery. For more than ten years, they searched for the perfect property, eventually finding eighty acres in the foothills overlooking the Napa Valley, of which thirty-five are now planted to Cabernet grapes.

The Wurteles wanted their new home to reflect California's heritage, convey an appreciation of contemporary art, and serve as a family retreat. Casa Cabernet, designed by Ricardo Legorreta, Mexico's internationally acclaimed architect, achieves all three goals. Legorreta's design aesthetic emerges from Mexico whose mystery, beauty, and humanity are revealed in the simple masses of its vernacular architecture. He reinterprets those forms and uses striking colors in a modern idiom, embracing emotion and intuition as valuable components of design. For the Wurteles, he called on his love of the vernacular to create an intimate and casual, yet serene and spacious house, perfectly suited to their needs. The commission became an intensely personal one for Legorreta, who made frequent site visits to refine the architecture and interior design and consult with Brooks Walker of Walker

At the hilltop site, Casa Cabernet, painted the earthy red of a fine vintage, rambles easily up the wooded slope. The entrance features natural materials, such as local stone for retaining walls and naturally spherical boulders in the front garden, and honey-toned wood on the garage door, that integrate the estate with the spectacular wooded setting.

Left: From the living room, a large, open gallery space that also serves as a covered patio has a panoramic view of the valley. Interior design by Legorreta that includes custom made furniture and sculpture and paintings by Mexican artists such as Tomayo perfectly harmonizes the inner space with the exterior.

Below: The asymmetry of the kitchen is emphasized by its open design adjacent to the entryway. From the living room, over-sized windows above the sink afford a continuous view of Margaret's vegetable garden and the hillside planted with California natives.

Warner Associates in San Francisco, who managed the construction.

The strong architecture required perfectly integrated landscaping. Landscape architect Jack Chandler, of Jack Chandler and Associates in Yountville, is pleased with the collaboration with Legorreta. "We share the same design aesthetic," he explains. "We're stylistically compatible, and that's important for a well-coordinated effort to create a complete whole."

Legorreta's design of three volumes set back into the forest allowed Chandler to respect the natural beauty of the evergreen woods. He created a minimalist South-western theme in the open areas, using low-maintenance, native California plantings to produce a sympathetic design for the residence. There is also an intimate vegetable garden for Margaret, a writer who has used the garden as metaphor in her work.

Legorreta works with his entire being and the full force of his heritage. Although striking color often dominates his work, walls are of primary significance for him. They define the interior and exterior spaces, give scale and proportion to the volumes, and integrate other elements such as color, light and shadow, and even water into the composition, giving it an identifiable character. The genius of Legorreta shines in the perfect composition for the

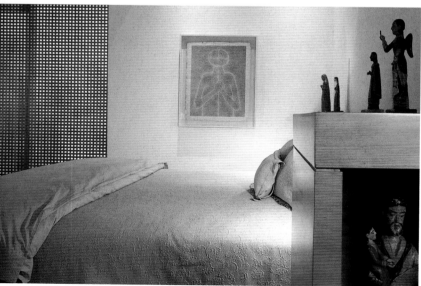

site, and he believes he succeeds if his clients become emotionally engaged with the space. The Wurtele retreat is now alive with creative endeavors, including publication of Margaret's two books, *Taking Root* and *Touching the Edge*, Angus's devotion to his vineyards, and happy visits with far-flung family members who now include a first granddaughter.

Residence of Angus and Margaret Wurtele, 1998
Ricardo Legorreta, Architect

Top left: Legorreta's clean design for the interior includes a substantial use of fine wood, in structural and decorative elements as well as for all of the furnishings. Large ceiling beams, cabinetry, and flooring of hardwoods stained a natural shade, complement the warm ivory-colored walls.

Bottom left: In the main bedroom, an ingenious perforated wooden screen becomes an outstanding design element while filtering the intense sunlight, and a collection of wooden Santos bless the owners' sleep.

Right: In the afternoon, the articulated fenestration in the dining room creates a dynamic pattern of shadows on Legorreta's expansive table. High back chairs continue the visual interplay of verticality and horizontality.

Following pages: A vineyard view of the Napa Valley.

ACKNOWLEDGMENTS

This book is dedicated to my friends Carter Lowrie and Bill Ryan, my husband David, and the inspiring Robert and Margrit Mondavi.

Carter and Bill are San Francisco residents and adventurous travelers who find joy in sharing experiences with their many friends and make life a festive occasion. It was over a decade ago that I day-tripped with them for my first visit to the Napa Valley. I am extremely appreciative of our friendship and their generosity of spirit.

My husband, David Pashley continually supports my creative efforts with his love and concern. His insights and care are invaluable.

Robert and Margrit Mondavi are bright and shining stars. Their palpable energy and charisma charmed me the moment I met them, and they continue to live lives of creativity and generosity that raise the bar for us all.

I would like to thank Steven Brooke, the energetic and mindful photographer whose beautiful work graces the pages of this book. It was an invigorating and inspiring experience to work with such a talented professional and driven artist whose life and aspirations always run in high gear. I feel fortunate to have met him.

Rizzoli's Senior Editor of Architecture, David Morton, is always the backbone of my projects. His considerate demeanor, kind suggestions, thoughtful insights and guidance, and humorous asides make the hours, days, months, and years of producing the final work an absolute joy.

Also at Rizzoli, Douglas Curran, Assistant Editor, is always helpful and diplomatic during the production of the book, and a pleasure to work with. Designer Abigail Sturges has again, as with *Santa Barbara Style,* produced a fantastic design that I think gives a perfect sense of the spirit of the place, in this case, the magical Napa Valley.

In the city of Napa, Nancy Lochmann, General Manager of the four-star Napa River Inn at the Historic Hatt Building, was particularly helpful and gracious. The ambiance of the Inn was exceptional and the Renaissance of downtown Napa was exciting to experience.

The homeowners of the Napa Valley whose properties were included in this book, and also those whose properties happen not to have been included, were some of the most spirited and creative people I have ever met. Their welcoming attitudes and generosity were much appreciated and marveled at. My hope is that this book vividly expresses their liveliness and joy.

A special thanks to Austin and Erika Hills, to Louise Newquist, and to Shannon Kuleto for their generosity and enthusiasm, particularly during the photographic shoots. It is a pleasure to know these festive people.

Many design professionals, business owners, non-profit historical organizations, researchers, and administrators contributed their expertise to this project. I thank the individuals and organizations listed below for their willingness to share their time, knowledge, and enthusiastic support. I am greatly appreciative, for without their help this book would not have been possible.

Stanley Abercrombie and Paul Vieyra, Sonoma
Tony S. Banthutham, Manager, Ca'Toga Galleria D'Arte, Calistoga
Thomas and Melina Bartlett, Napa
Andrew Batey, Architect and Gina Martel, Rutherford
Bill Belloli and John Hodges, San Francisco
Beringer Winery and Vineyards, St. Helena
Ron and Joann Birtcher, Napa
Paul Bonacci and Lucinda Schlaffer, ARQ Architects, San Francisco
Diane Burns, Interior Designer, New York City, New York
California Partners in Flight
Jack Chandler, Chandler & Associates Landscape Architecture, Yountville
Daphne Churbuck, Graham Eliot Interior Design, Osterville, Massachusetts
Gertrude Colgin, Tychson Hill, St. Helena
Monty Collins, Monty Collins Interior Design, St. Helena, San Francisco, Seattle
Dennis Copeland, Archivist and Historian, California History Room, Monterey Public Library, Monterey
COPIA: The American Center for Wine, Food & the Arts
Ronald Cox, Napa Construction Company, Napa
K.C. and Jerry Cunningham, Napa Valley Opera House, Napa
Rene di Rosa, The di Rosa Preserve, (Carneros) Napa
Leslie Erickson, Business Manager; Susan Powers Kennelly, Public Relations and Spokesperson Board Member: Napa County Landmarks, Inc., Napa
Kate Firestone, owner, Firestone Winery, Santa Barbara
Flavia Peppinella del Foculare, Napa
Hope Fowler, Culpeper, Virginia
Ken Fulk and Kurt Wootton, historic Sampson House, Napa
Brian Fuller, Manager, Ira Yeager Studios, San Francisco and Calistoga
Patricia Gebhard, author, Santa Barbara

Tim Guetzlaff, Interior Designer, TMG & Associates, St. Helena
Steve Guttenberg, Honorary Mayor, Pacific Palisades
Hendrix-Allerdyce, Illya Hendrix and Thomas G. Allerdyce, Interior Design, Los Angeles
Joanna Hess, Santa Fe, New Mexico
Jorgen and Marion Hildebrandt, Calistoga
Richard Hilkert, Bookseller, San Francisco
Ericka Hills, Ericka Hills Antiques, St. Helena
Carla Howard, Producer, Marin
Laura Jernigan and Judy Troppmann, Sweetie Pies, Napa River Inn, Napa
Edward Keiner, Architect, Keiner & Kaston, Napa
The Kreiss Family, Calistoga
Shannon Kuleto, Food and Wine Historian, Kuleto Estate Family Vineyards
Jennifer La Liberté, Project Coordinator, City of Napa Redevelopment/Economic Development Department
The Lenzo Family, Rutherford
Ricardo Legorreta, architect, Mexico City and Los Angeles
Nancy Lochmann, General Manager; Monty Sanders, Communications; Napa River Inn and Hatt Building Marketplace, Napa
Carter West Lowrie, Society of Decorative Arts, San Francisco
Ken and Kathy Macke, Oakville
Orville Magoon, President, Winegrower; Karen Magoon, Owner; Leah Wake, Public Relations; Joann Schwartz, Hospitality: Guenoc-Langtry Estate Vineyards & Winery, Middletown, Napa and Lake Counties
Louise Mann, Louise Mann Interior Design, San Francisco
Suzanne Martinson, Architect, Miami, Florida
Martha and Tom May
Robert and Margrit Mondavi, Oakville
Monterey County Historical Society
Frances and Esme Morris, Delaplane, Virginia
Napa Chamber of Commerce, Napa
Napa County Historical Society, Napa
Napa County Landmarks, Inc., Napa
Napa Valley Opera House and Margrit Biever Mondavi Opera Theatre Company, Napa
Napa Valley Shakespeare Festival, Napa
Napa River Inn and Hatt Building Marketplace, Napa
Louise Newquist, Board of Directors, di Rosa Preserve, Napa
Barbara Niemann, Rutherford
David Pashley, Vice President Conservation Programs, American Bird Conservancy, The Plains, Virginia
Alex and Robert Phillips, Napa
Armando Rascon, Peter Wright Gallery, San Francisco
Mary Raimondi, Curatorial Department; Richie Sorenson, Rights and Reproductions; Fiona Griffin, Assistant in Registrar's Office: Smithsonian Art Museum, Washington D.C.

The Reid Family, Napa

Carol Romano, Interior Designer and Textile Importer, San Miguel de Allende, Mexico

Susie and Leslie Rudd, St. Helena

William Ryan, William Ryan Communications, Inc., San Francisco

John Sanders, Department of Public Affairs, Naval Post-Graduate School, Monterey

Michael Savage, Executive Director, Napa Valley Opera House and Margrit Biever Mondavi Opera Theatre Company, Napa

C. Terence Schell, Interior Designer, San Francisco

Larry and Lauren Seese, Calistoga

Sharpsteen Museum, Calistoga

Andrew Skurman, Architect, Andrew Skurman Architects, San Francisco

Allison Lane Simpson, Director of Public Relations, Beringer Winery, St. Helena

Kristin Smith, Collections Assistant, National Portrait Gallery, Smithsonian Institute, Washington D.C.

Ned and Dorothy Soderholm, Napa County Historical Society, Napa

Jeff Steen, Owner, Pacific Blues Café, Yountville

Frank and Suzette Stephenson, Proprietors, Boar's Breath Restaurant & Oven, Middletown

Norm and Norma Stone, Calistoga

Tim Thomas, Historian, History and Arts Association of Monterey and Monterey Maritime Museum, Monterey

Brandon Tyson, Garden Design, Napa

Jeff Van Houten, Historian, Beringer Winery, St. Helena

Edward and Marilyn Wallis, Calistoga

Wine Train of Napa, Napa

John York, Historian, Chairman of Napa County Planning Commission, St. Helena

RESOURCES

Allegra, Antonia. *Napa Valley the Ultimate Winery Guide.* San Francisco: Chronicle Books, 2000

Archuleta, Kay. *The Brannan Saga: Early-day Calistoga.* San Jose: Smith McKay Printing Co., 1977

Barron, Cheryll Aimee. *Dreamers of the Valley of Plenty: A Portrait of the Napa Valley.* New York: Scribner, 1995

Bell, Ian. *Dreams of Exile: Robert Louis Stevenson, A Biography.* New York: Henry Holt and Company, 1995

California Partners in Flight and S. Zack. *The Oak Woodland Bird Conservation Plan: A Strategy for Protecting and Managing Oak Woodland Habitats and Associated Birds in California.* Stinson Beach: Point Reyes Bird Observatory, 2002

Caldewey, Jeffrey. *Wine Tour: Napa Valley.* San Francisco: The Wine Appreciation Guild, 1988

Chappellet, Molly with Richard Tracy. *Gardens of the Wine Country.* San Francisco: Chronicle Books, 1998

Conaway, James. *Napa: The Story of an American Eden.* Boston: Houghton Mifflin Company, 1990

Daily, Gretchen C. and Katherine Ellison. *The New Economy of Nature: The Quest to Make Conservation Profitable.* Washington, Covelo, London: Island Press, 2002

Dillon, Richard H. *Napa Valley's Natives.* Napa: James Stevenson Publisher, Napa County Historical Society, 2001

Duchscherer, Paul. *The Bungalow: America's Arts & Crafts Home.* New York: Penguin Books USA, Inc., 1995

_____. *Inside The Bungalow: America's Arts & Crafts Interior.* New York: Penguin Putnam Inc., 1997

Gleeson, Bill. *Backroad Wineries of Northern California: A Scenic Tour of California's Country Wineries.* San Francisco: Chronicle Books, 1994

Halberstadt, April. *Bungalow Style.* New York: Michael Friedman Publishing Group, Inc., 2000

Halliday, James. *Wine Atlas of California.* New York: Penguin Group, Penguin Books USA, Inc., 1993

Haynes, Irene W. *Ghost Wineries of Napa Valley.* San Francisco: The Wine Appreciation Guild, 1995

Heintz, William. *California's Napa Valley: One Hundred Sixty Years of Wine Making.* San Francisco: Scottwall Associates, 1999

Hitchmough, Wendy. *The Arts & Crafts Lifestyle.* New York: Watson-Guptill Publications, 2000

Howell, Patton (Edited by). *Napa Valley.* Dallas, Texas: Saybrook Publishing Co., Inc., 2000

Issler, Anne Roller. *Stevenson at Silverado: The Life and Writing of Robert Louis Stevenson in the Napa Valley, California, 1880.* Fairfield, California:

James Stevenson Publisher, Napa County Historical Society, 1996

James, George Wharton. *The Old Franciscan Missions of California.* Boston: Little, Brown, and Company, 1915

Kilgallin, Anthony Raymond. *Images of America: Napa: An Architectural Walking Tour.* Chicago, Illinois: Arcadia Publishing, Tempus Publishing, Inc., 2001

Kirker, Harold. *California's Architectural Frontier: Style and Tradition in the Nineteenth Century.* Salt Lake City: Gibbs M. Smith, Inc., 1986

Laube, James. "Rethinking Napa Valley." *Wine Spectator.* Pp. 36-70. New York: M. Shanken Communications, Inc., February 29, 2000

Locke, Juliane Poirier. *Vineyards in the Watershed: Sustainable Winegrowing in Napa County.* Napa: Napa Sustainable Winegrowing Group, 2002

Marchiori, Carlo. *Testa Veneziana a Ca' Toga: The Imaginative World of a Venetian Artist in Napa Valley.* Berkeley: Ten Speed Press, 2002

Mondavi, Robert with Paul Chutkow. *Harvests of Joy: My Passion for Excellence.* New York: Harcourt Brace & Company, 1998

Mondavi, Robert, Margrit Biever Mondavi, and Carolyn Dille. *Seasons of the Vineyard: Celebrations and Recipes from the Robert Mondavi Winery.* New York: Simon & Schuster, 1996

Napa Community Redevelopment Agency. "A Vision for Historic Downtown Napa." Napa: City of Napa, 1999

Napa Community Redevelopment *Agency. Traditions of the Past: Visions for the Future: The Downtown Napa Renaissance.* Napa: City of Napa, 2001

Napa County Flood Control and Water Conservation District. *Progress and Plan Summary 2002.* Napa: Napa County Flood Control and Water Conservation District, 2002

Napa County Landmarks, Inc. *Landmark News,* Vol. 20, No. 2. Napa: Napa County Landmarks, Inc., Summer 2002

Napa Valley Museum. *Ira Yeager: A Retrospective Exhibition.* Yountville: Napa Valley Museum, 1999

Nordhoff, Charles. *California for Travellers and Settlers.* Berkeley: Ten Speed Press, 1974

Porterfield, Meredie Dozier. "Charles Krug & His Winery," *Gleanings,* Vol. 4, No. 3. Napa: Napa County Historical Society, 1990

_____. "George Yount: His Fur Trapping Years," *Gleanings,* Vol. 4, No. 1. Napa: Napa County Historical Society, 1988

Prchal, Dolly. "Josephine Marlin Tychson: The First Woman Winemaker in California," *Gleanings,* Vol. 3, No. 4. Napa: Napa County Historical Society, 1986

Prial, Frank J. *Decantations: Reflections on Wine by The New York Times Wine Critic.* New York: St. Martin's Press, 2001

Robinson, W.W. *Land in California: The Story of*

Mission Lands, Ranchos, Squatters, Mining Claims, Railroad Grants, Land Scrip, Homesteads. Berkeley, Los Angeles, London: University of California Press, 1979

Schoenfeld, Bruce. "Napa Valley Epic." *Wine Spectator.* Pp. 40-54. New York: M. Shanken Communications, Inc., June 15, 2000.
_____. "Napa Mavericks." *Wine Spectator.* Pp. 38-52. New York: M. Shanken Communications, Inc., July 31, 2002

Soderholm, E.P. Ned. *20,000 Years of Transportation to the Napa Valley: Local History Sketch No. 12.* Napa: Napa County Historical Society, 1992
_____. *Some Napa County Highlights: Local History Sketch No. 14.* Napa: Napa County Historical Society, 2000

Sparks, Drew and Sally Kellman. *A Salon at Larkmead: A Charmed Life in the Napa Valley.* Berkeley: Ten Speed Press, 2000

Starr, Kevin. *Inventing the Dream: California through the Progressive Era.* New York: Oxford University Press, 1985

Stevenson, Robert Louis. *The Silverado Squatters.* New York: Charles Scribner's Sons, 1897; St. Helena: The Silverado Museum, 1974

The Oakland Museum. *The Arts and Crafts Movement in California: Living the Good Life.* New York: Abbeville Press Publishers, 1993

Tinniswood, Adrian. *The Arts & Crafts House.* New York: Watson-Guptill Publications, 1999

Weber, Lin. *Old Napa Valley: The History to 1900.* St. Helena: Wine Ventures Publishing, 1998
_____. *Roots of the Present: Napa Valley 1900 to 1950.* St. Helena: Wine Ventures Publishing, 2001

Wemyss, Nina. (Edited by). *Soul of the Vine: Wine in Literature: A Selection.* Oakville: Robert Mondavi Winery, 1999

Wichels, John. *George C. Yount on Caymus Rancho 1836-1865: Local History Sketch, Series 3, No. 1.* Napa: Napa County Historical Society, 1980

Wright, Elizabeth Cyrus. *The Early Upper Napa Valley.* Originally published in 1949. Republished: Calistoga, California: Sharpsteen Museum, 1991

INDEX

Left and above: Interior designs by
Daphne Churbuck, of Graham Eliot in
Massachusetts, blend a traditional sensi-
bility with a playful color palette that
heightens the effect of sunlight.

CALIFORNIA RANCH HOUSE